BLACK & DECKER ®

WIRING

101

25 Projects You _Really_ Can Do Yourself

JODIE CARTER

Creative Publishing
international

Copyright © 2006
Creative Publishing international, Inc.
18705 Lake Drive East
Chanhassen, Minnesota 55317
1-800-328-3895
www.creativepub.com
All rights reserved

Printed in Singapore

10 9 8 7 6 5 4 3 2 1

President/CEO: Ken Fund
Vice President/Retail Sales & Marketing:
  Kevin Haas

Executive Editor: Bryan Trandem

Author: Jodie Carter
Editor: Andrew Karre
Art Director: David Schelitzche
Cover Design: Howard Grossman
Book Design: Richard Oriolo
Page Layout: Kari Johnston
Assistant Managing Editor: Tracy Stanley
Photo Acquisitions Editor: Julie Caruso
Production Manager: Linda Halls

NOTICE TO READERS

For safety, use caution, care and good judgment when following the procedures described in this book. The Publisher and
Black & Decker cannot assume responsibility for any damage
to property or injury to persons as a result of misuse of the
information provided.

The techniques shown in this book are general techniques for
various applications. In some instances, additional techniques
not shown in this book may be required. Always follow manufacturers' instructions included with products, since deviating
from the directions may void warranties. The projects in this
book vary widely as to skill levels required: some may not be
appropriate for all do-it-yourselfers, and some may require professional help.

Consult your local Building Department for information on
building permits, codes and other laws as they apply to your
project.

CONTENTS

Welcome to Wiring

WIRING 101 REPRESENTS A DIFFERENT TYPE OF HOME REPAIR BOOK: YOU DON'T NEED TO HAVE ANY PRIOR KNOWLEDGE TO BE SUCCESSFUL. ALMOST EVERY HOME REPAIR BOOK DEPENDS ON YOU HAVING SOME FAMILIARITY WITH THE SUBJECT MATTER BEFORE YOU BEGIN. IF YOU HAPPEN TO BE A TRUE BEGINNER, YOU'RE ALREADY AT A DISADVANTAGE.

What do you do, then, if you have no idea exactly what an electrical circuit is, if you don't really know the difference between wire strippers and needlenose pliers? What if you don't know that the thing you've always called an "outlet" is really a receptacle, and if you have no idea of the difference between a circuit breaker and a fuse?

You reach for Wiring 101. This is the one book on electrical wiring that doesn't assume you already know a lot about the subject. But it's also a book that won't insult your intelligence and talk down to you.

Professional electricians tell us that 95 percent of all service calls involve just a few basic repairs, so chances are you really don't need a book that teaches you how to rewire your entire house. What you do need is a book that shows you the 25 most common projects you're likely to face, a book that describes the projects in careful, no-step-left-out detail, so you can get the job done with no problem.

On the following pages, that is exactly what you'll find: directions for solving the 25 universal wiring problems and projects in your home. No knowledge is assumed, and no question is left unanswered.

Despite what you might think, or what you might fear, you really don't need a lot of technical understanding to have success at most wiring projects. Of course, it's great if you understand things like the "polarity of alternating current," or the difference between a short circuit and a ground fault, but the fact is that you don't need to know these things to replace a wall switch that buzzes, or to replace an ordinary outdoor floodlight with one that senses motion and turns on automatically to make the shadows safer when you're coming home late at night.

Wiring is a whole lot easier than most people think, because when it gets right down to it, electricity behaves in very logical, predictable ways. If you make repairs in a systematic way that carefully follows the proper steps, wiring is simpler than most plumbing or carpentry projects.

With that in mind, many of the projects in this book are extremely basic. There are just a few pages devoted to learning how to make wire connections, or how a circuit works. The rest is all practical step-by-step information, beginning with the most basic of projects. (Yes, we actually do show you how to remove a broken lightbulb.) And we'll show you how to put a new plug on the end of your toaster or lamp cord. And how to replace a lamp cord that has worn through. Surprisingly, these routine problems are ignored in many wiring books. There are also more substantial projects here, such as replacing wall switches and receptacle outlets. And at the end of the book, you'll find a couple of "extra credit" projects—how to install track lighting in replacement of an ordinary ceiling-mounted light fixture, and how to add new electrical outlets with surface-mounted raceways. Although these projects are a bit more advanced, you'll be happy to find that they're easier than you imagined. From the skills you learn with these 25 projects, you'll develop the confidence you need to do almost any wiring project that comes along.

HERE'S HOW TO USE THIS BOOK:

The first two pages of each project give you the background information and any technical understanding that will be helpful to understanding what you're about to do. You'll learn about the skills required, get an idea of how long the project might take, and see all the tools and materials you'll need to gather to do a project.

Then, turn the page and begin. Virtually every step is photographed so you'll see exactly how to do the work, and along the way you'll find helpful sidebars that show you what to do if something unexpected happens, tips for using tools correctly, safety recommendations, and more. Before you know it, you'll notch up another home repair success.

It's that easy. Really.

Electrical tape

Toolbox

viper
ROUTER BITS

Wire connectors

Lamp cord

Westinghouse
8' LAMP CORD SET

Lamp sockets

Switches & receptacles

SPT-1 Wire

Screwdrivers

Current sensor

Needlenose pliers

Combination tool

WIRE STRIPPER A.W.G.

WIRE CUTTER

Here's pretty much all you'll need to complete most of the repairs and projects in this book. They are available at any home improvement center or hardware store.

UNLIKE SOME OTHER TYPES OF HOME IMPROVEMENT SKILLS, MAKING BASIC wiring repairs doesn't require very much at all in the way of tools and materials. Investing $30 to $40 puts you in a position to save hundreds of dollars on routine wiring repairs. We recommend that you keep a small toolbox with items dedicated to your wiring tools. That way, you can bring your kit to your work site, and will have the screwdrivers, pliers, and other things you need handy, and won't have to hunt for a screwdriver at the most inconvenient time. Here are the things we recommend for your wiring tool kit:

• **Electrical tape.** These days, tape isn't used to make wire connections, but to help label wires temporarily as you replace fixtures. Some electricians, though, do wrap a loop of electrical tape around plastic wire connectors to reinforce the connections.

• **Toolbox.** A small plastic toolbox is just fine; one with a divided tray for holding wire connectors, screws and other small items is a good choice.

• **Wire connectors.** Sometimes known as "wire nuts," after one manufacturer's product. They're used to join wires together, and you'll be using them a lot. They're color coded for convenience. Green connectors are used for bare copper grounding wires. With most manufacturers, orange connectors are used for two small wires, yellow for two or three wires, red for three or more wires. But you should follow the recommendations on the box, in case you buy a different brand.

• **Lamp sockets.** Repairs to lamps and light fixtures are very common, so you can save yourself time by having a few of these on hand. Besides, they're very inexpensive.

• **Switches & receptacles.** Because these are so frequently needed, and so inexpensive, keep a few on hand. Sooner or later, you'll need them.

• **Cord kit.** Another inexpensive item that's good to have on hand. Lamp cord kits have preattached plugs, to make rewiring a lamp very easy.

• **Screwdrivers.** Have at least two screwdrivers; one with a slot-shaped tip, the other with an X-shaped Phillips tip. It's even better to have several sizes of each type.

• **Needlenose pliers.** This tool is used for almost every wiring project, and is used mostly for bending and connecting wires.

• **Current sensor.** This clever tool tells you if the wires you want to work on are carrying electricity or not. Best of all, this new-style tool doesn't require that you touch any wires.

• **Combination tool.** This workhorse does it all: cuts cables, identifies wire sizes, strips wires. It is the single most important wiring tool you can have.

There are handful of other workshop tools you may use in your wiring projects. They include: a portable drill, a hammer, a level, a utility knife, a tape measure, and a stud finder. If you don't already own them, you may need to buy or borrow them when you get to projects that require them.

Before You Begin: Understanding an Electrical Circuit

NO QUESTION ABOUT IT: WIRING AND ELECTRICITY MAKE MOST PEOPLE JUST A LITTLE NERVOUS. Understanding a bit about how electricity behaves in the wires that run through your house will help take away a bit of the scary mystery, and will also give you some confidence to make these repairs. So let's take a short tour of your electrical system. You might even carry the book along with as you walk through your home looking for the things we describe.

Electricity is really nothing more than a form of magnetism running through wires. Electrical energy is obviously invisible, but it's useful to think of it in much the same way as you'd think about water flowing through plumbing pipes. Like water, the electricity is present but not really moving until you "open the faucet" by turning on a light switch, or turning on the motor for an appliance.

Problems occur when the wires (the "pipes") carrying current become broken or blocked, or if they "leak" electricity outside the system. If you're ever been shocked, you know one result of electricity leaking outside its wires. Because flowing electricity generates heat, leaking electricity can also cause fires. These are the reasons electricity makes people a little nervous: it's an invisible energy, it can cause shocks, and it can cause fires.

Fortunately, the system has lots of safety features built in to prevent these problems. And to stay perfectly safe while making repairs to the system, all that's necessary is for you to shut off the flow of electricity in the wires you want a work on. This is very, very easy to do, as you'll soon see. Let's start the tour:

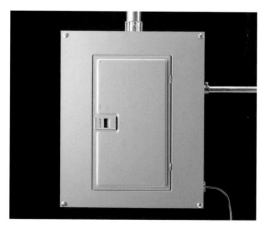

1 For all intents and purposes, your electrical system begins for you with the **main service panel.** Usually this is a gray metal box located in a utility area of your home—the basement, the garage, or a utility room. Sometimes, though, it might be located inside a wooden wall cabinet in a finished basement room.

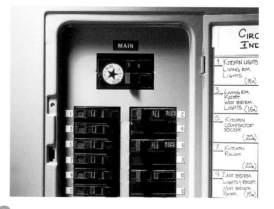

2 Inside the service panel are rows of toggle switches. These are **circuit breakers**. They serve two functions. First, they protect wires from having too much current flowing through them. If you've ever had a circuit breaker trip and lights go out suddenly, you've experienced this safety feature. Secondly, the circuit breakers let you shut off the power to wires when you want to work on them.

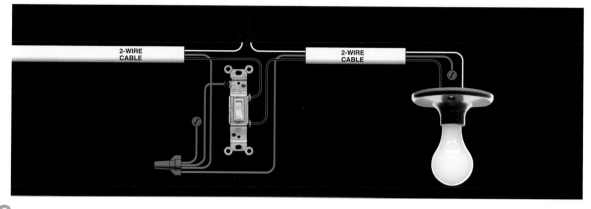

3 Each of the circuit breakers in the service panel sends and controls electricity through a **circuit**—a continuous loop of wire that runs from the service panel, out to one or more receptacles, appliances, or light fixtures, and back again. This diagram shows a simplified circuit. Even the most complicated circuits are just variations of this basic idea. Electricity changes its nature as it flows through the circuit wires. It begins as **"hot" current**.

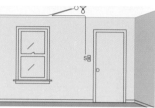

This current is under **"pressure,"** which means that it carries voltage. After the electricity does its work, by creating light or heat or moving mechnical parts in an appliance, it loses its pressure, or charge, and becomes **"neutral"** as it flows back to the service panel. The wires carrying hot current are normally black or red, while neutral wires are usually white. In addition to the hot and neutral wires, a circuit has a loop of bare copper wire (or sometimes an insulated green wire). This **grounding wire** is a safety feature that carries stray electricity back to the service panel if the other wires "leak" their electricity.

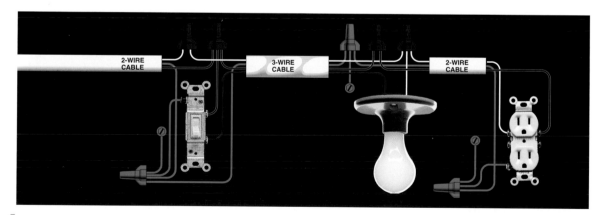

4 Here's another circuit map that shows how a more complicated circuit works. This circuit sends electricity to both a switch/light combination, and a receptacle outlet. If you follow the path of the black wire, you'll see how it works. As the black wire carrying hot current reaches the switch location, it branches, sending one black wire that passes all the way through the light fixture and goes to the receptacle. This allows the receptacle to operate

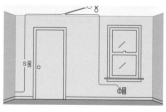

independently from the switch and light. Back at the switch, you'll see that another black wire leads to the switch. The hot current passes through the switch, then is carried to the light fixture through a red wire, which is part of a cable containing three insulated wires. From both the light fixture and the receptacle, white wires carry "depressurized" neutral current back to the service panel.

Before You Begin:
Turning Off the Power

1 Find your main service panel (see page 8). Make sure there is no moisture on the floor below the panel. In very rare instances, people have been shocked when they touch a service panel while standing in water. Open the door of the panel, and look for the index on the inside face of the door. If your electrical service has been properly mapped, the index will tell you exactly which circuit breaker controls the circuit wires you want to work on. This isn't always the case, though. Sometimes you'll need to switch them off one at a time, identifying the correct breaker through trial and error.

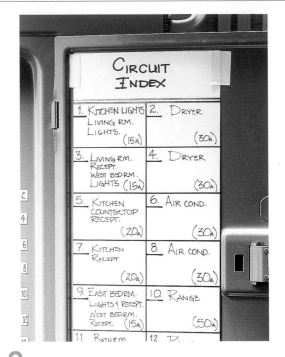

2 With your finger, snap the lever on the circuit breaker to the OFF position. You will hear an audible click, and on some breakers a red window will appear on the face of the breaker. Now, close the panel door, and make very sure that everyone in the house knows you'll be working on wires, and that they shouldn't touch the service panel. **DO NOT** actually work on wires until you've tested for current (next page).

WHAT IF...?

If you have an older home with an electrical panel that contains fuses rather than circuit breakers, you will shut off power to the circuits by removing the fuses.

1 Locate the fuse that controls the circuit wires you plan to work on. Like a circuit breaker panel, fuse panels usually have an index that labels the circuits. The circuits that control ordinary wall outlets and light fixtures are usually screw-in fuses. The fuses for large appliances are usually cartridge fuses that fit into a fuse block you pull out of the panel.

2 Unscrew the fuse, being careful to touch only the insulated rim of the fuse.

Before You Begin: Testing for Current

No-touch current testers are very easy to use, but they are accurate only if they are working properly. Before trusting it to test wires to make sure they are safe to work on, test the tool on a fixture that is carrying live current—the power cord on a lamp that is turned on, for example. Turn the tester to ON, then move the probe around the lamp wires until the tester glows or sounds its audible alarm. Now you know the tool works correctly, and can trust it to accurately test wires for live current.

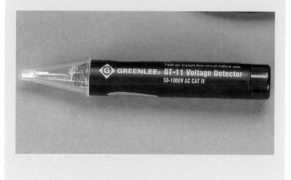

Receptacles: Remove the coverplate on the receptacle. Turn the tester on, and verify it works by testing it on wires you know to be live. Now insert the probe tip on the receptacle into the electrical box on each side of the receptacle. If the tester does not indicate current, you know the wires are now safe to work on.

Light fixtures: Loosen mounting screws and carefully lower the light fixture away from the ceiling box. With the wall switch in the ON position, pass the tip of the current tester within ½" of each wire.

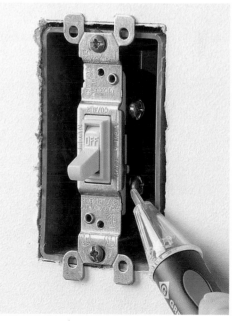

Wall switches: Remove the coverplate on the switch, and insert the tip of the current tester into the box, passing it within ½" of each of the screw terminals on the side of the switch. If the tester does not light up or beep, the wires are safe to work on.

Before You Begin:
Making Wire Connections

ONE OF THE FEW SKILLS THAT IS UNIVERSAL TO MOST WIRING PROJECTS IS STRIPPING WIRES OF THEIR OUTER PLASTIC JACKETS, exposing the bare wires, and then connecting those wires to each other or to wire leads or screw connectors on switches, outlet receptacles, light fixtures, or other devices. So before moving on to any actual repairs in this book, practice the following skills:

- Stripping cables and wires
- Connecting wires
- Making screw terminal connections
- Making push-in connections
- Making set-screw connections

HOW TO STRIP WIRES

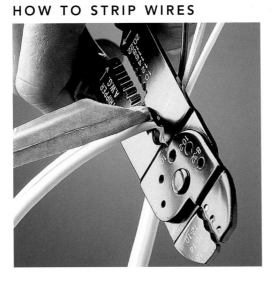

1 If you need to, cut away any plastic sheathing on the cable containing the wires, using the cutting jaws of a combination tool, or a utility knife. (If you use a utility knife, make sure not to nick the plastic jacket on the individual wires. If necessary, you can trim the wires down to size, using the cutting jaws on the combination tool.

3 To strip insulation from the individual wire, select the opening on the combination tool that matches the size of the wires. In most instances, you'll be using the 12-gauge or 14-gauge openings on the tool. Open the jaws and place the wire in the correct slot, then close the jaws of the tool around it. Tug on the wire until it comes free from the insulation.

2 Determine how much wire to strip. Many receptacles and other devices come with a gauge that tells you how much wire to strip. Usually, it's about ¾".

HOW TO CONNECT WIRES WITH SCREW CONNECTORS

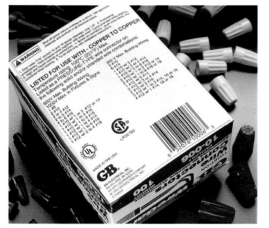

1 Screw connectors are used to join circuit wires together, or to join circuit wires to the wire leads on a light fixture, dimmer switch or other device. Choose a wire connector appropriate for the number of wires you're connecting, and for their size. Wire connector packages come with recommendations for usage. Green wire connectors are reserved for grounding wires.

2 Hold the wires together and slide a wire connector onto them. Twist clockwise until the wires are snug. You shouldn't be able to see any bare wire exposed. Tug on the wires gently to make sure they're firmly attached.

HOW TO MAKE SCREW TERMINAL CONNECTIONS

1 Strip about ¾" of insulation from each wire, using your combination tool. Choose the slot in the tool that corresponds to the wire size—this will almost always be 14-gauge or 12-gauge wire for the type of wiring you're doing.

2 Form a C-shaped loop in the end of the wire, using a needlenose pliers. Make sure the wire has no nicks or deep scratches. If it does, clip it off and restrip the ends of the wire.

3 Hook each wire around the appropriate screw terminal on the device, so it forms a clockwise loop. Attach only one wire under each screw terminal. Tighten the screw securely. The plastic insulation on the wire should just touch the screw, and the end of the wire should be under the screw, not extending beyond it.

HOW TO MAKE PUSH-IN CONNECTIONS

1 Although they are not as secure as screw connections, you can also use push-in connections on some switches. Some devices also have push-in connections. To make this connection, use the strip gauge on the back of the device to mark the wire for stripping. Use a combination tool to strip the wire.

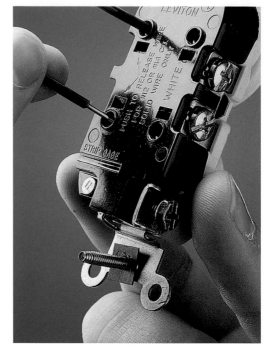

2 Insert the bare copper wires firmly into the push-in fittings on the back of the switch or receptacle. There shouldn't be any bare wire exposed. Tug gently to make sure the wire is firmly gripped. If not, remove the wire and reinsert. If the device won't grip the wire tightly, connect the wire using the screw terminals instead.

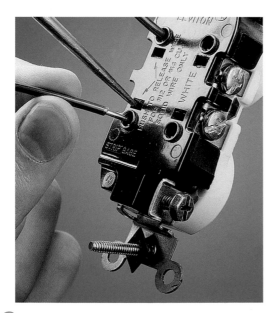

3 If you need to remove a wire from a push-in fitting, insert a small nail or screwdriver into the release opening next to the wire. The wire should pull out easily.

WHAT IF...?

A new type of wire connector looks like a twist connector, but instead uses a simple push-in action. Strip the wires to the length indicated, then simply slide the bare wires into the holes on the connector.

A continuity tester is a specialty tool that can be used to test lamp cords, switches, sockets, switches, and other devices to see if they are working correctly. The continuity tester is a battery-operated tool that sends a very faint electrical current through the metal components on a device, and senses whether or not there is a continuous pathway for household current to follow. If you have doubts about the condition of a device, the continuity tester offers a quick way to tell if the device is faulty or not.

Although there's only one project in this book that calls for a continuity tester, it's useful tool you might want to add to your wiring tool kit.

On lamp cords, use the continuity tester to check the pathway from the prongs on the plug to the ends of the cords.

On pull-chain switches, attach the clip of the tester to one of the switch leads, and hold the tester to the other lead. Pull the chain. If the switch is good, the tester will glow when the switch is in one position, but not in the other.

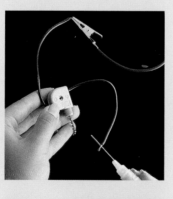

On wall switches, attach the clip of the tester to one of the screw terminals and touch the probe to the other screw. Flip the switch lever from ON to OFF. If the switch is good, the tester will glow when the switch is ON, but not when OFF.

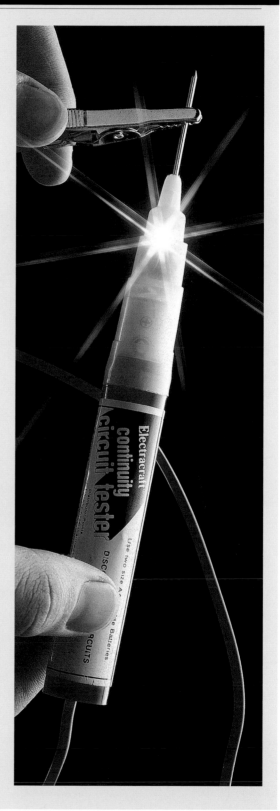

Adding a Wireless Phone Jack

1

Wireless phone jack systems make it posssible to add telephone jacks without running new phone cable through walls. In a matter of moments, you can add a phone jack wherever you have an electrical outlet.

HOME CENTERS AND ELECTRONICS STORES SELL "WIRELESS" PHONE JACK KITS that use your household electrical wiring to transmit phone signals. The kits include two pieces. One is a base unit you plug in to a standard electrical receptacle and then connect to a standard phone jack. This provides a bridge between the phone wires and the electrical system. The second piece is the wireless jack, which you can plug in to any electrical receptacle in the house. To create additional phone jacks, just buy more wire jack units from the same manufacturer. Kits are sold for around $50, with extra jacks costing $20 to $30.

HOW TO ADD A
WIRELESS PHONE JACK

1 Purchase a wireless phone jack kit. Most come with one base unit (A) and one wireless jack (B), which will allow you to add a phone jack anywhere you have an electrical receptacle.

Use the included length of phone wire (C) to connect the base unit to an existing phone jack near an electrical receptacle. You can plug the cord into either of the two jacks on the transceiver. The other jack lets you plug in a phone.

2 Plug the wireless jack in any electrical receptacle in the house or garage, provided it is part of the same electrical system. Plug your phone into the jack on the side of the unit.

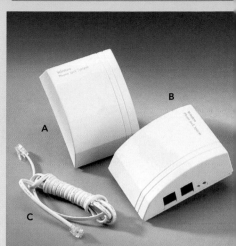
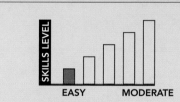
WHAT IF...?

If you want to use a computer modem with a wireless jack, consider buying a wireless model designed for high-speed modem connections. Although all wireless units can be used with computer modems, they transmit at a rate of 14.4K or so. Wireless jacks designed for computer modems, on the other hand, transmit at 56K.

2

Repairing Phone Jacks

Phone jacks are easily damaged. Whether they get smashed by an errant chair leg or their wires get rattled loose, a faulty jack can degrade the quality of the sound on your phone—or disconnect you altogether. The good news is that working on phone wiring is easy and very safe.

REPAIRING OR REPLACING A BROKEN PHONE JACK is a project that offers a lot of bang for the buck. If a phone jack somewhere in your house has stopped working or has very poor sound quality, you can probably fix it by investing $5 and less than an hour of your time.

The phone system is separate from the household wiring, and runs on a very mild current, which means you don't have to worry about shock. You don't have to turn anything off to replace a phone jack.

PHONE JACKS 101

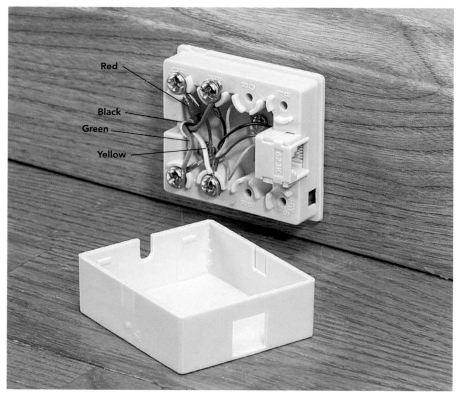

Red
Black
Green
Yellow

Phone jacks generally have four thin colored wires in them. The wires are connected to screw terminals or to slotted brackets. The four wires are usually colored red, yellow, green and black. Connect the individual system wires to the screw or bracket connected to the matching color leads leading to the modular plug.

CHEAT SHEET

If your wires don't match the color scheme shown here, don't worry. Use this chart as a reference for connecting wires to the screw terminals:

The red terminal will accept:
- a red wire
- a blue wire (or blue with white stripe)

The green terminal will accept:
- a green wire
- a white wire with blue stripe

The yellow terminal will accept:
- a yellow wire
- an orange wire (or orange with white stripe)

The black terminal will accept:
- a black wire
- a white wire with orange stripe

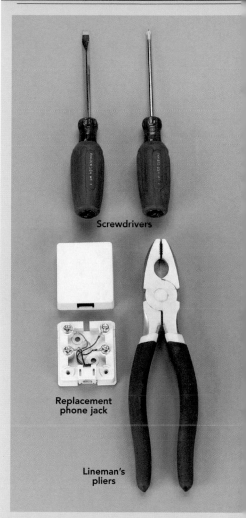

Screwdrivers

Replacement phone jack

Lineman's pliers

SKILLS YOU'LL NEED

- Making wire connections (page 12)

DIFFICULTY LEVEL

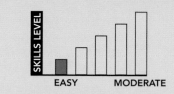

SKILLS LEVEL

EASY   MODERATE

You'll likely finish this in 30 minutes or less.

HOW TO REPAIR A PHONE JACK

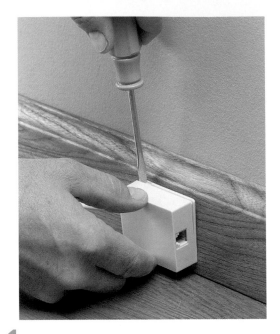

1 If the jack has no visible damage, you may be able to get it working again by reconnecting loose wires inside. Pry the cover off the jack with a small screwdriver.

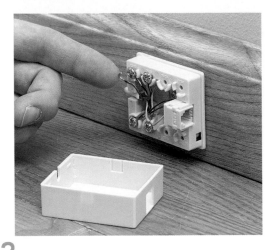

2 Under the cover, you'll see six or eight wires in four colors. Each of the wires should be firmly seated under a screw terminal or in a forked metal tab. If one of the wires is loose, reattach it to the terminal of matching color. Plug in the phone to test it. If it still doesn't work, continue with replacing the jack

3 To remove the jack, first disconnect all the wires from their screw terminals or forked tabs. Then, unscrew the screws (there may be one or two) holding the jack to the wall. Tape the phone wires to the wall so they don't get knocked into the wall cavity.

4 Take the old jack to a hardware store or home center and try to find a similar replacement jack so you can use the same mounting holes. Remove the cover from the new jack. Carefully thread the phone wire through the back of the new jack, and connect the wires to the screw terminals of matching color. Attach the jack to the wall, replace the cover, and test the phone

What if I have a *really* old jack? Older style phones used a four-pin system rather than modular plugs. New phones won't work with these jacks, so you'll need to replace them with new modular jacks.

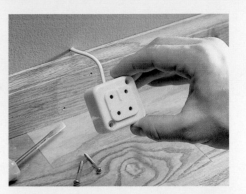

1 Unscrew the old jack from the wall, and carefully pull it away from the wall.

2 On the back of the old jack, you'll find two or four colored wires connected to screws. Unscrew the screws to free the wires and then clip away the stripped portion of the wires. Buy a new modular phone jack.

3 If your new jack uses forked tab connectors, thread the phone cable through the opening in the back of the jack, then press each of the four wires into a forked tab that already contains a wire of the same color running to the plug-in opening. If your new jack uses screw terminals, follow the instructions on the opposite page. After all the wires are connected, plug in a phone. You should have a clear dial tone.

4 Set the jack over the old mounting holes and make sure the wire isn't being pinched against the wall. Drive the mounting screws back into the holes. Snap the cover back onto the jack and plug in your phone.

3

Removing a Broken Lightbulb

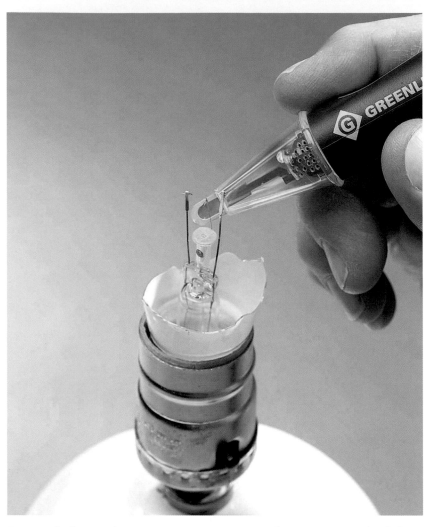

Even with the simplest wiring repairs, using a voltage sensor to check for power is a good idea. We'll then show you how the pros handle this job— using a needlenose pliers to remove the broken lightbulb. This technique works on even the most corroded and rusted light fixture sockets.

IF YOU'VE EVER TRIED TO REMOVE A LIGHTBULB THAT'S CORRODED AND STUCK in a fixture socket, you know that the lightbulb can easily break, leaving the bulb's aluminum base stuck in the fixture. There are several solutions to this common problem; some work better than others. For example, you may have heard of the old potato trick that suggests you push a raw potato into the broken socket and turn. But this introduces moisture and other debris into the fixture, and it doesn't work that well, especially if your broken bulb is really stuck. The bar of soap technique isn't much better. Effective methods include using a pair of needlenose pliers or a bulb extractor device, which can be found at most hardware or home improvement stores.

LIGHT SOCKETS 101

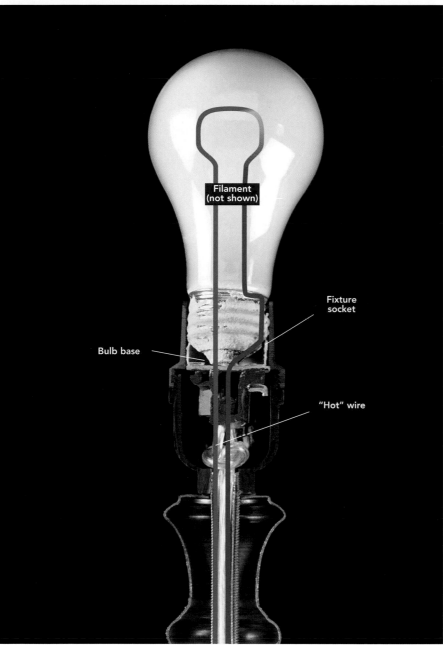

Filament
(not shown)

Fixture
socket

Bulb base

"Hot" wire

Over time, the aluminum base of a lightbulb may become corroded and difficult to remove from its socket. You can almost always remove the bulb without damaging the socket. In this cutaway lamp, you can see exactly how a light fixture socket works. Current flows up into the lightbulb through the "hot" wire and through the central contact in the base of the bulb. The current flows through the filament inside the light bulb, loses its charge by producing light, then the neutral current flows back to the neutral wire through the threaded metal portion of the bulb and socket.

TOOLS & SUPPLIES YOU'LL NEED

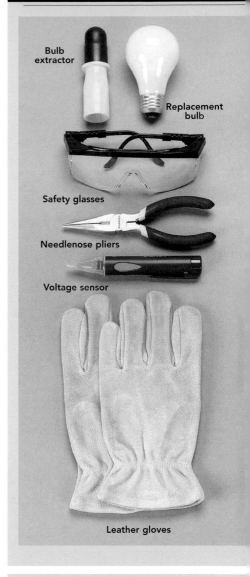

Bulb
extractor

Replacement
bulb

Safety glasses

Needlenose pliers

Voltage sensor

Leather gloves

SKILLS YOU'LL NEED

- Turning off the power (page 10)
- Testing for current (page 11)

DIFFICULTY LEVEL

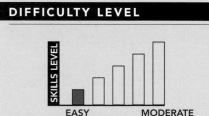

SKILLS LEVEL

EASY   MODERATE

You'll finish this job in just a few minutes.

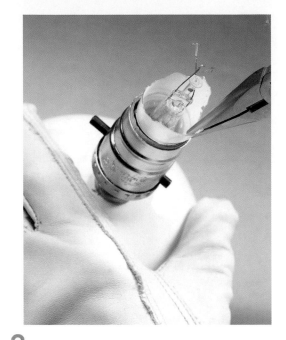

1 Before you start to remove the broken bulb, turn off the power to the light (or unplug the lamp, if that's what you're working on). Then, with the light switch in the ON position, place the tip of your voltage sensor in the broken bulb base. If the sensor beeps or lights up, then the wires are still live and are not safe to work. Check the main circuit panel again and trip the correct breaker to disconnect power to the light. If the sensor does not beep or light up, the circuit is dead and safe to work on.

2 Put on safety glasses and a pair of heavy leather work gloves. Use your needlenose pliers to remove any broken shards of glass still attached to the lightbulb base. If you're working on a ladder, have a helper hold the base of the ladder.

TOOL TIP

Needlenose pliers are handy for all sorts of household repairs, not just wiring. They come in all sorts of sizes. A good basic pair should have jaws around 3" long and comfortable handles.

3 Insert the needlenose pliers into the broken bulb base as far as they will go. Spread the handles of the pliers firmly apart (this will cause the jaws to press against the inside of the socket), and turn the pliers slowly counterclockwise, unscrewing the bulb base. If the bulb won't budge, try wrapping the jaws of the pliers in duct tape for extra grip.

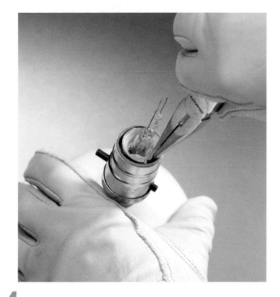

4 If the lamp is still stuck, use the tip of needle-nose pliers to grab the lip of the bulb base and bend it in slightly on one side. Grip the bent portion firmly with the pliers, and pull the base counter clockwise to unscrew the bulb.

5 If the broken bulb is in a hard-to-reach location or if you're not comfortable working on top of a ladder, you can buy a broken bulb extractor (available at hardware stores for less than $10) and screw it on to the end of a broom handle or extension pole. Simply insert the extractor into the socket. Its rubber sides grip the edge of the bulb base and give enough grip to allow you to turn the base out of the socket.

WHAT IF...?

What if the bulb still won't turn?

The base of the bulb is soft aluminum, and, if you pull hard enough, it will begin to tear much like a pop can. If you can't twist the bulb out, you may be able to create a little tear in the edge of the base. Try to fold the tear back. You'll probably rip a piece of the bulb off. Eventually, you'll have the whole socket out.

6 Once the bulb is out, wipe away any corrosion in the socket with a rag. If bulbs often get stuck in a particular fixture, use a bulb socket lubricant (available at hardware stores) to lubricate the lightbulb base and prevent corrosion. And remember, there's no need to twist hard when installing a bulb.

Controlling Lights
From a Keychain Remote

4

Remote kits include a plug-in receiver unit (left) and a keychain remote (right).
Some models include multiple transceivers that let you connect several lamps
or other plug-in appliances.

A KEYCHAIN REMOTE IS A VERY EASY WAY TO IMPROVE YOUR PERSONAL SAFE-
TY FOR AN INVESTMENT OF ABOUT $20. It lets you turn on a lamp before you enter a
dark home, or to leave it on until you're safely in your car. The receiver module plugs into
any household outlet. Plug a lamp into the bottom of the receiver, and you can control the
light with the keychain remote.

HOW TO SET UP A KEYCHAIN REMOTE

1 Plug the receiver into the receptacle where you usually plug in the lamp you want to control. Open the cover panel on the unit. There will be two dials, one with a "unit code" (typically a number) and another with a "house code" (typically a letter). If you're only planning on controlling one device, any code will do.

3 Plug the lamp into the unit and switch the lamp on. Test the remote by turning the lamp on and off.

2 Set the small switch below the dials to "learn." Hold one of the "on" buttons on the keychain down until the light on the unit flashes. The keychain is now programmed for this unit.

SKILLS YOU'LL NEED

• Reading package directions

DIFFICULTY LEVEL

Very easy; takes just a few minutes.

5

Different appliances and lamps have different kinds of plugs. In all cases, replacing a damaged plug is an easy task, once you identify which replacement plug you need. Appliances and tools often have thick, round cords (A, B) and heavy plugs, sometimes with three-prong plugs. Small appliances and lamps often use small plastic plugs (C, D). Some devices use "polarized" plugs (E) which have one wide prong and one narrow prong. Polarized plugs can only be plugged into a receptacle only one way.

ELECTRICAL PLUGS ARE SIMPLE DEVICES THAT TAKE A LOT OF ABUSE, and, not surprisingly, they often break at inconvenient times. You can almost always replace the plug for a tiny fraction of the cost of replacing the appliance or device. Replacing a badly bent or crushed plug can prevent a bad shock or even a fire.

PLUGS 101

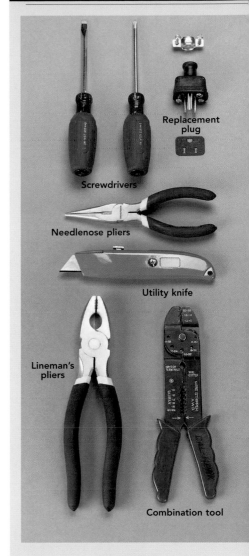

Replacement plug

Screwdrivers

Needlenose pliers

Utility knife

Lineman's pliers

Combination tool

SKILLS YOU'LL NEED

• Making wire connections (page 12)

DIFFICULTY LEVEL

SKILLS LEVEL

EASY   MODERATE

You'll need 15 to 20 minutes for this.

Appliances, lamps, and other electrical devices generally have plugs with either two or three prongs. The round third prong on a three-prong plug provides a path into the grounding system in your home. Receptacles in older homes might not be designed for three-prong plugs, requiring you to use an adapter (see page 33). When replacing a plug, always choose one that resembles the original.

HOW TO REPLACE A THREE-PRONG PLUG

1 Use lineman's pliers to cut off the old plug. Cut as close to the base of the plug as possible. Take the old plug with you to a hardware store or home center and purchase an identical replacement plug.

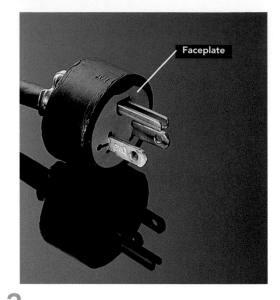

Faceplate

2 Pry the plastic faceplate off the front of the replacement plug with a small screwdriver.

3 Feed the cut end of the cord through the rear of the plug so that you have about three inches of the cord coming through the front of the plug. Use a sharp knife to carefully cut the plastic insulation off the cord. Then, use your combination tool to strip about ¾" of insulation from the ends of each of the three insulated wires inside the cord.

4 Next, you'll need to tie an underwriter's knot with the black and white wires where they emerge from the plug. (See the opposite page.) This knot prevents the wires from coming loose inside the plug.

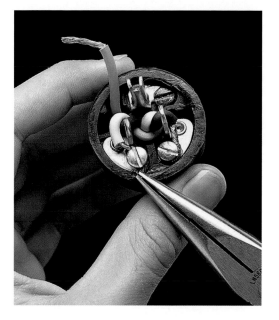

5 Now you'll need to connect the wires to the plug. On the face of the plug, you'll see three screws, one silver, one copper-colored, and a third green. Loosen the silver screw a few turns and wrap the end of the white wire clockwise around the screw. Needlenose pliers can make this easier. Tighten the screw, making sure the bare wire doesn't touch either of the other screws. Then, connect the black wire to the copper screw in the same way. Finally, connect the green wire to the green screw. When all the wires are secure, snap the faceplate into place and test the cord.

HERE'S HOW

To keep wires secure in the plug, tie a special knot in the white and black wires, called an underwriter's knot.

Create loops in each wire outwards from the cord, then feed the end of each wire through the opposite wire's loop—white through the black loop, black through the white.

Now pull the wires tightly, closing the loops and completing the underwriter's knot.

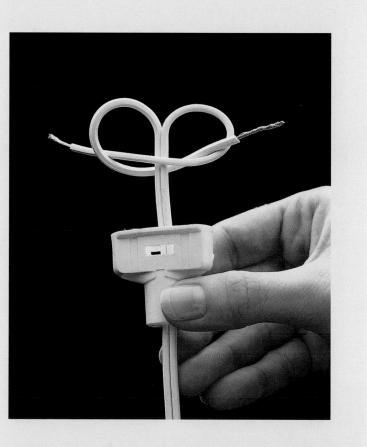

HOW TO REPLACE A TWO-PRONG PLUG

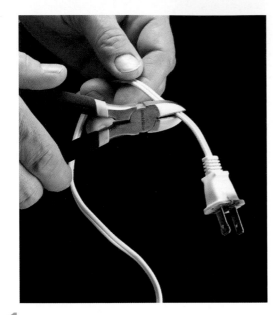

1 Use lineman's pliers to cut off the old plug. Cut as close to the base of the plug as possible and make your cut perpendicular to the cord.

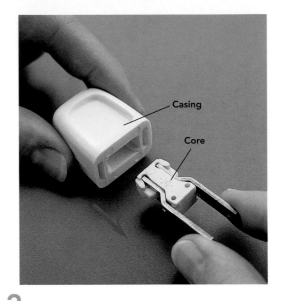

2 The quick-connect replacement plug has two parts, an outer casing and a core. Squeeze the prongs of the plug together and pull the core out of the casing.

Casing

Core

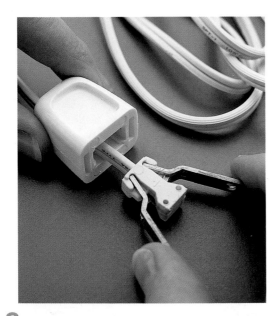

3 Feed the cut end of the cord through the quick-connect plug's casing. Spread the prongs on the core and then push the end of the cord into the back of the core. Firmly squeeze the prongs together. You should feel two small spikes on the insides of the prongs pierce the cord's insulation. Slide the core back into the casing. The casing will hold the prongs in place. Now you can test the plug.

WHAT IF...?

What if your appliance has a polarized plug?

If the plug you're replacing had a wide prong and a narrow prong, you'll need to purchase a similar quick-connect replacement plug. When you assemble the plug, make sure the wide prong of the plug lines up with the ribbed half of the cord. The wide prong is the neutral, and will only fit into the neutral slot on a wall receptacle.

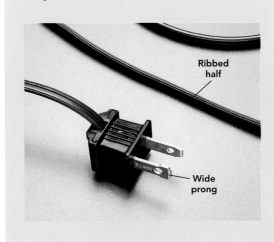

Ribbed half

Wide prong

HOW TO REPLACE A FLAT-CORD PLUG

1 Cut the old plug from the cord, using a combination tool. Pull apart the two halves of the cord so that about 2" of wire is separated. Strip ¾" of insulation from each half. Remove the casing cover on the new plug.

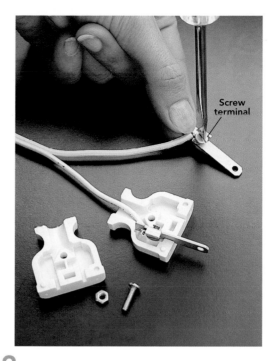

2 Hook the ends of the wires clockwise around the screw terminals, and tighten the screw terminals securely. Reassemble the plug casing. Install the insulating faceplate, if the plug has one.

SAFETY TIP

What if your home has only two-slot receptacles and you need to use an appliance with a three-prong plug?

NEVER break off the third prong. Instead, use a grounding adapter. Make sure to attach the metal loop on the adapter to the coverplate screw on the receptacle.

A better long-term solution will be to replace this receptacle with a three-slot receptacle that is properly grounded. Turn to project 12 on page 62 if you'd like to try this.

Fixing a Doorbell

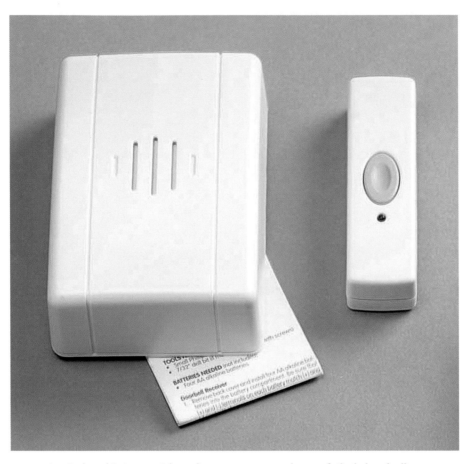

6

A wireless kit is a quick and easy way to replace a failed doorbell system. The kit consists of a battery-powered doorbell button that sends a wireless signal to a plug-in chime unit somewhere in the house. Some models come with two button units, one for the front door and one for the back.

WHAT DO YOU DO IF YOUR DOORBELL DOESN'T CHIME? The repair may be as simple as repairing loose wires or replacing a $2 button. The most common causes of doorball malfunction—loose wiring and worn-out buttons—are the easiest to fix, requiring only a screwdriver.

If the problem is with the wiring itself or the chime unit, it's generally simpler and cheaper to replace the system with a wireless doorbell kit, which take only minutes to install and cost very little.

DOORBELLS 101

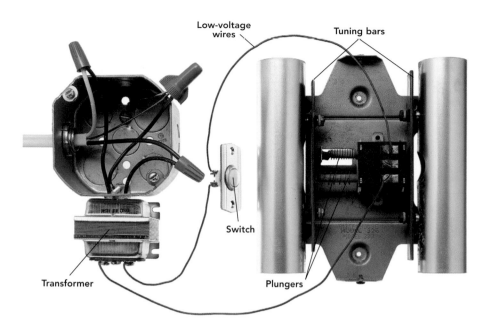

Low-voltage wires

Tuning bars

Switch

Transformer

Plungers

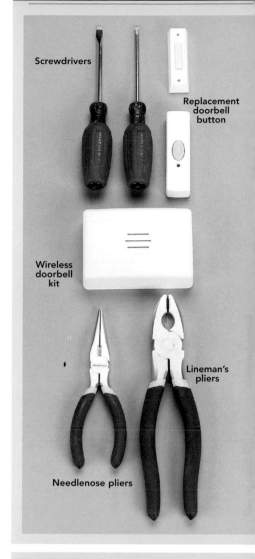

Screwdrivers

Replacement doorbell button

Wireless doorbell kit

Lineman's pliers

Needlenose pliers

Repairing or replacing a doorbell is a simple project that often doesn't even require you to shut off the power. Doorbells are powered by a transformer that reduces household current to 24 volts or less. This low-voltage current goes from the transformer to the switch by the door and on to a chime unit. When you press the doorbell button, it completes a low-voltage pathway and causes the plunger to strike a musical tuning bar. To distinguish between the front and back door signals, one of the doorbell switch-and-plunger pairs strikes two tuning bars in succession, creating the characteristic "ding-dong" sound. The other switch and plunger strikes only one tuning bar.

SKILLS YOU'LL NEED

• Turning off the power (page 10)

• Testing for power (page 11)

• Making wire connections (page 12)

HERE'S HOW

Rarely, it may be a loose wire connection on the doorbell chime unit that causes the problem. Remove the cover on the chime unit, look for loose wires, and tighten them with a screwdriver. More often, though, the problem will be with the push-button switch, or with a chime unit that has simply reached the end of its life.

DIFFICULTY LEVEL

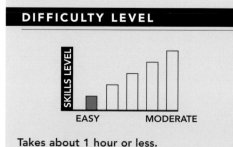

SKILLS LEVEL

EASY   MODERATE

Takes about 1 hour or less.

1 Begin by testing the button to make sure it works. Doorbell buttons are commonly the culprit. Use a screwdriver to remove the two screws that secure the doorbell cover to the house.

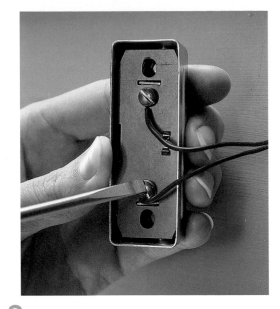

2 Carefully pull the switch away from the wall. Check the two wire connections on the back of the switch. If the wires are loose, reconnect them to the screws on the back of the button. Test the doorbell by pressing the button. Check the two wire connections on the back of the switch. If the wires are loose, reconnect them to the screws on the back of the button. Test the doorbell by pressing the button.

3 If the doorbell still doesn't work, loosen the screws on the back of the doorbell, remove the wires, and touch their bare copper ends together. If the bell sounds, the problem is a faulty button you'll need to replace (go to step 4). If the bell doesn't sound, the problem is elsewhere in the system (go to step 5). If you're replacing the switch, disconnect the wires and tape them to the wall to keep them from falling inside and getting lost.

4 To replace the switch, simply buy a replacement that has the mounting holes in the same location as the old one. Wrap each of the wires around one of the screws on the back of the switch and tighten the screws. Position the button over the mounting holes and attach the new button to the wall with a screwdriver.

5 If the bell didn't ring, check the transformer, which is probably located in the basement or utility room near your main service panel. Check the two wires connected to the surface of the transformer, and reconnect them if they're loose. Test the doorbell by pressing the button. If the doorbell still doesn't sound, go to step 6.

6 If nothing else has worked, now it's time to install a new wireless doorbell kit. First, plug in the chime unit to a centrally located receptacle in your house. Disconnect the doorbell switch by your door, and clip off the wires as close to the wall as possible, using lineman's pliers.

7 Install the battery into the battery compartment of the doorbell button. Go outside your front door and press the button to make sure the chime rings. If not, you may need to move the indoor receiver to a receptacle closer to the door.

8 Mount the button to the door frame where you removed the old doorbell. You may have to drill two new holes before securing the new button to the wall with screws. Some doorbells come with double-sided tape that can be used to secure the button to the wall or to door molding. Push the doorbell button to make sure it works.

Fixing a Lamp Socket

7

Fixing an old lamp is a satisfying and surprisingly simple process. No matter what a lamp looks like on the outside, they almost always have the same electrical components.

WHEN A LAMP STOPS WORKING, IT'S OFTEN CAUSED BY A BAD LIGHTBULB SOCKET UNIT—that's the piece containing the switch or pull chain that holds the lightbulb. No need to throw the lamp away: for a few dollars, you can replace the socket and restore the lamp to like new. Replacing a socket is easy, and most hardware stores and home centers sell a variety of replacement sockets.

LAMP SOCKETS 101

Lamp sockets and switches are usually interchangeable—choose whatever type you want. Included here from top left: twist knob, remote switch, pull chain, push lever.

TOOLS & SUPPLIES YOU'LL NEED

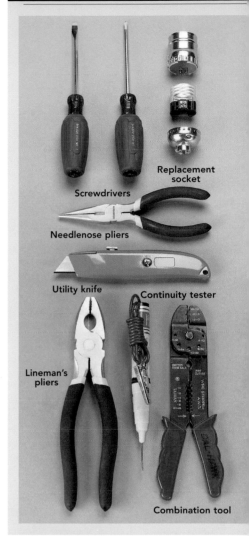

Screwdrivers

Replacement socket

Needlenose pliers

Utility knife

Continuity tester

Lineman's pliers

Combination tool

QUICK FIX

Sometimes, you'll get lucky and you can fix the faulty socket very easily. With the lamp unplugged and its bulb and shade removed, use a small flat screwdriver to pry up the small metal tab on the base of the socket. The tab should be angled slightly upward, not pressed flat in the socket. If the tab doesn't touch the base of the bulb, electricity will not flow though the bulb. Prying it up may restore the current flow. Replace the bulb and test the lamp.

Contact tab

SKILLS YOU'LL NEED

- Stripping and connecting wires (pages 12 and 13)
- Testing for continuity (page 15)

DIFFICULTY LEVEL

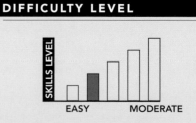

SKILLS LEVEL

EASY   MODERATE

This job takes 30 to 60 minutes.

Outer shell

Insulated sleeve

1 With the lamp unplugged, the shade off, and the bulb out, you can remove the socket. Squeeze the outer shell of the socket just above the base and pull the shell out of the base (the shell is often marked "Press" at some point along its perimeter. Press there and then pull).

3 With the shell and insulation set aside, pull the socket away from the lamp (it will still be connected to the cord). Look at the two screws on the sides of the socket. One half of the cord should be connected securely to each. If the screws are loose or if either of the wires is unattached, you've found the problem. Reconnect the ends of the cord and tighten the screws. But if the connections seem sound, then you'll need to continue by unscrewing the two screws to disconnect the socket.

2 Under the outer shell, you'll find a cardboard insulating sleeve. Pull this off and you'll reveal the socket attached to the end of the cord.

WHAT IF...?

What if my lamp is old and the shell is held in place by screws?

Some older lamps may have an outer shell held together with small screws. Simply undo the screws, remove the outer shell, and proceed as described here.

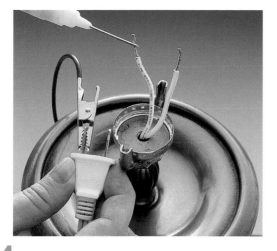

4 To rule out a bad cord as the cause of the problem, attach the clip of your continuity tester to one prong of the lamp's plug; then touch the probe first to one of the bare wires and then to the other. Do the same test for the other prong. The tester should light up once for each prong. If the tester never lights or lights on both wires for the same prong, you'll need to replace the cord (see pages 30 to 33). If it lights up once for each prong, the socket is the problem.

5 Attach the ribbed half of the wire to the silver screw terminal on the new socket. Attach the other wire to the brass-colored screw terminal. If the stripped ends of the cord are frayed or blackened, cut them off with your combination tool and strip away ¾" of insulation to reveal clean wire.

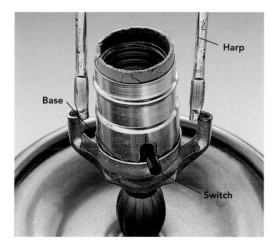

Harp

Base

Switch

6 Set the socket on the base of the lamp. Make sure the switch isn't blocked by the "harp"— the part that holds the shade on some lamps. Slide the cardboard insulating sleeve over the socket, so the sleeve's notch aligns with the switch. Now slide the outer sleeve over the socket, aligning the notch with the switch. It should snap into the base securely. Screw in a lightbulb, plug the lamp in, and test it.

HERE'S HOW

Here's how to buy a replacement socket. First, make sure it accepts the same size bulb (you'll be able to see this by looking). Next, if your old socket has a twist-, push-, or pull-chain-style switch, find a replacement that has the same style. (If the socket doesn't have a switch, you'll need to find a socket without one.) Finally, make sure it has the same watt rating as the old socket. Somewhere on the inside or outside of the socket, you'll find a number (between 20 and 120) followed by a *W*. This is the watt rating.

Replacing a Lamp Cord

8

Lamp cords get lots of abuse, so it's not uncommon for them to wear out. A damaged cord is a major fire and shock hazard and just wrapping it with electrical tape is not a safe repair technique. Fortunately, replacing a cord is fairly simple and much cheaper than replacing the lamp.

LAMP CORDS ARE BASICALLY ALL ALIKE, no matter what the lamp looks like. They disappear into the base of the lamp, snake through the lamp, and end at the socket where the bulb screws in, simple as that. Replacing one requires only disconnecting the damaged cord from the socket and then snaking the new cord back through the lamp to the socket.

LAMP CORDS 101

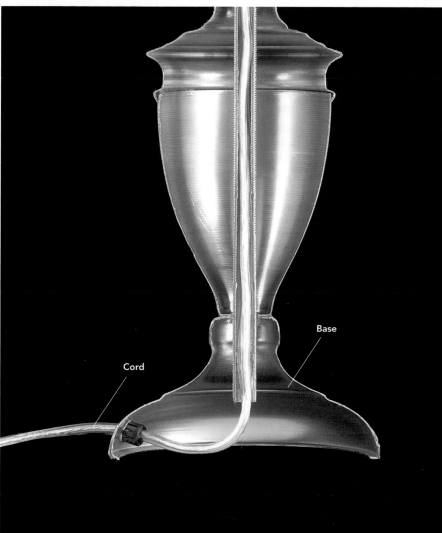

Cord

Base

Table and floor lamps are actually pretty simple. The cord runs from the base of the lamp up to the socket (which often houses the switch). If there's a problem with a lamp, it's likely either with the cord or the socket (project #7).

WHAT IF...?

What if you have a big floor lamp? It will be easier to snake the new cord into the lamp with a little help from the old one. A couple inches from the base of the lamp, cut the old cord. Tape the bare end of the new cord to the end of the old cord. Now, you pull the new cord into the lamp by pulling out the old cord through the top.

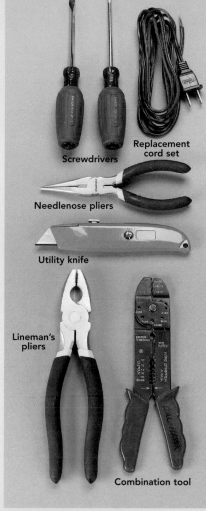

Screwdrivers

Replacement cord set

Needlenose pliers

Utility knife

Lineman's pliers

Combination tool

SKILLS YOU'LL NEED

• Making wire connections (page 12)

DIFFICULTY LEVEL

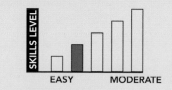

SKILLS LEVEL

EASY   MODERATE

This repair takes about 1 hour.

HOW TO REPLACE A LAMP CORD

1 With the lamp unplugged, the shade off, and the bulb out, you can remove the socket. Squeeze the outer shell of the socket just above the base and pull the shell out of the base (the shell is often marked "Press" at some point along its perimeter. Press there and then pull).

2 Under the outer shell, you'll find a cardboard insulating sleeve. Pull this off and you'll reveal the socket attached to the end of the cord.

3 With the shell and insulation set aside, pull the socket away from the lamp (it will still be connected to the cord). Unscrew the two screws to completely disconnect the socket from the cord. Set the socket aside with its shell (you'll need them to reassemble the lamp)

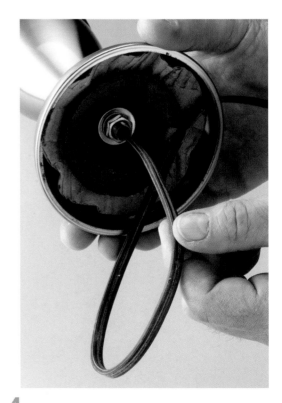

4 Remove the old cord from the lamp by grasping the cord near the base and pulling the cord though the lamp.

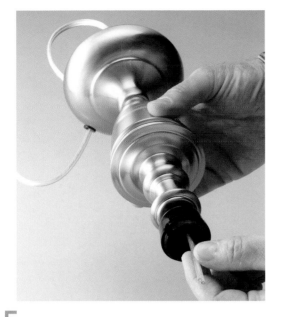

5 Take your damaged cord to a hardware store or home center and purchase a similar "cord set." (A cord set is simply a replacement cord with a plug already attached.) Snake the end of the cord up from the base of the lamp through the top so that about 3" of cord is visible above the top.

7 Connect the ends of the new cord to the two screws on the side of the socket (one of which will be silver in color, the other brass-colored). One half of the cord will have ribbing along its length; wrap that wire clockwise around the silver screw and tighten the screw. The other half of the cord will be smooth; wrap it around the copper screw and tighten the screw.

6 Carefully separate the two halves of the cord. If the halves won't pull apart, you can carefully make a cut in the middle with a knife. Strip away about ¾" of insulation from the end of each half.

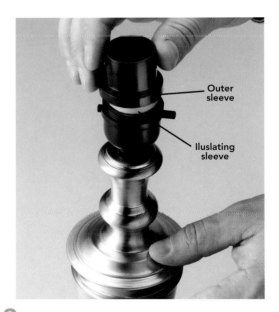

Outer sleeve

Iluslating sleeve

8 Set the socket on the base. Make sure the switch isn't blocked by the "harp"—the part that holds the shade on some lamps. Slide the cardboard insulating sleeve over the socket, so the sleeve's notch aligns with the switch. Now slide the outer sleeve over the socket, aligning the notch with the switch. It should snap into the base securely. Screw in a lightbulb, plug the lamp in, and test it.

9

Fixing a Pull-chain Switch

The pull-chain switch is actually a separate piece of the fixture. It's held in place with a retaining nut and connected to circuit wires with two wire leads.

CHANCES ARE YOU'VE GOT A LIGHT FIXTURE WITH A PULL-CHAIN somewhere in your house—in a closet, attic crawl space, or maybe even your bathrom vanity. And, chances are, if you use it enough, you will eventually pull a little too hard and the switch will fail. Fortunately, you can easily replace a pull-chain switch, generally for only a dollar or two.

This is the first project where you actually touch circuit wires, so make sure you read the information on shutting off power and testing for current, found at the beginning of this book.

PULL CHAINS 101

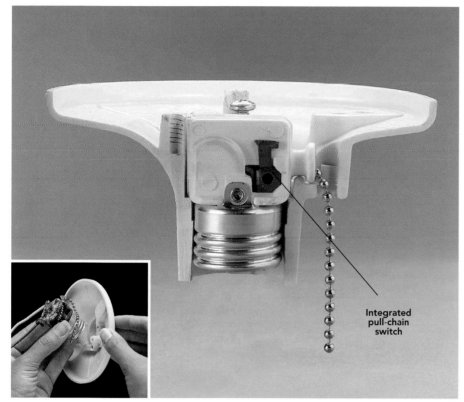

Integrated
pull-chain
switch

On some utility light fixtures, the pull-chain switch is part of the lightbulb
socket. On these fixtures, you'll need to replace the entire socket/switch
unit (inset).

TOOLS & SUPPLIES YOU'LL NEED

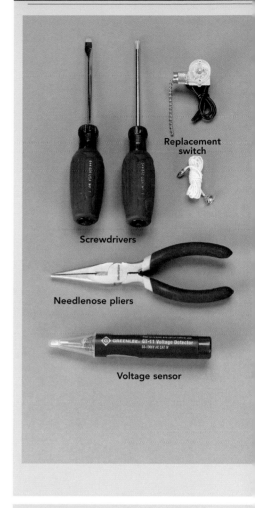

Replacement
switch

Screwdrivers

Needlenose pliers

Voltage sensor

WHAT IF...?

If you have a light fixture
or lamp with a push-button
switch, replacing the switch is
exactly the same as for a
pull-chain switch.

Just buy a replacement switch
that matches the old switch,
and replace it using the same
technique described on the
following pages.

SKILLS YOU'LL NEED

- Turning off the power (page 10)
- Testing for power (page 11)
- Making wire connections (page 12)

DIFFICULTY LEVEL

SKILLS LEVEL

EASY   MODERATE

This project takes less than 1 hour.

HOW TO REPLACE A PULL-CHAIN SWITCH

1 First, make sure that switch is broken, not just the chain. If you find a short bit of chain sticking out of the fixture, pull on it to see if the light turns on and off. If so, you can buy and attach a new length of pull chain. If there's no chain left or if the switch doesn't work when you pull the remaining chain, go ahead and replace the switch.

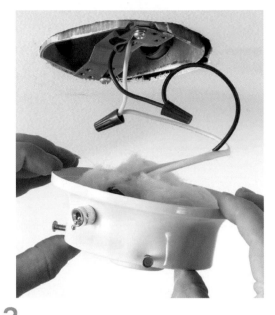

2 First, turn off the power to the fixture. Now, remove the globe and lightbulb, and loosen the mounting screws that hold the fixture to the electrical box. Lower the fixture away from the ceiling.

3 Test for current by holding your voltage sensor within ½" of the circuit wires. The black wires should cause the sensor to beep if power is present. Check all the wires for power in case the light was wired improperly. If the sensor beeps or lights up, then the circuit is still live and is not safe to work. Check the main circuit panel again and trip the correct breaker to disconnect power to the fixture. If the sensor does not beep or light up, the wires are dead and safe to work on.

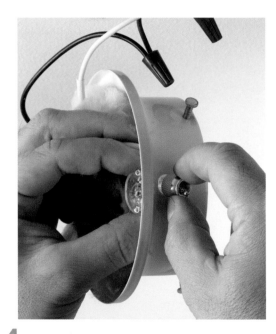

4 Hold the fixture steady with one hand and turn the knurled retaining nut at the base of the pull chain. You should be able to turn it with your fingers. If it sticks, use needlenose pliers to turn it. Once the retaining nut is off, pull the switch out of the fixture.

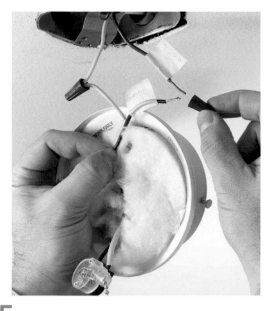

5 Remove the two wire leads coming from the switch from the wires they are attached to by unscrewing the wire connectors. On most fixtures, one of the switch's leads will be connected to a circuit wire, the other lead to the light fixture itself.

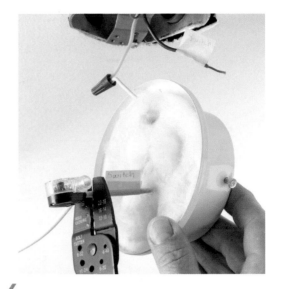

6 If the switch is part of the fixture itself, snip off its connection, using a combination tool. You'll connect the new switch to the wire you've just snipped, so strip about ¾" of insulation off that wire.

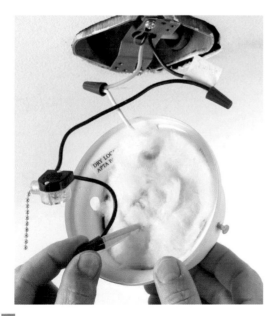

7 Attach the wire leads on the new switch to the disconnected wires, using wire connectors. Then, insert the threaded portion of the switch through the hole. Slip the retaining nut over the pull chain and thread it on to the switch until it is snug.

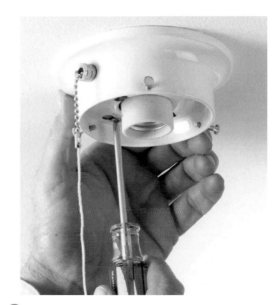

8 Reattach the fixture to the ceiling by holding it over the electrical box in the ceiling so that the mounting holes in the fixture line up with the screw holes in the box. Make sure all the wires are in the box and not pinched between the ceiling and the fixture. Insert the mounting screws and tighten them down with a screwdriver. Now you can replace the bulbs, restore the power, and test the fixture.

Installing a
Programmable Thermostat

10

Programmable thermostats come in many varieties, but all of them will help save on energy costs. Most models have instructions for programming printed on the access plate.

IF YOUR HOME'S TEMPERATURE IS CONTROLLED BY AN OLD DIAL-TYPE THERMOSTAT, you may want to replace it with a modern programmable thermostat, which can save you up to one-third on your heating and cooling costs. Programmable thermostats allow you to set temperature levels for different times of the day according to the schedules of those living in the house. For instance, in the winter, you can program the thermostat to turn the heat up to 73 degrees in the morning when you are waking up, automatically lower the temperature to 69 degrees during the day while you are gone, then raise the temperature back up to 73 degrees just before you arrive home in the evening, then lower back down to 69 degrees again while you are sleeping.

Prices range between $19 and $120 depending on the unit's features. Some thermostats offer different programming schedules, including a five-to-seven-day schedule. When shopping, keep in mind that you might want to program a slightly different schedule for every day of the week. In that case, make sure you purchase a seven-day programmable thermostat. Also, keep in mind that some of the lower-priced models may result in temperature variations of up to nine degrees. If in doubt, get help from a salesperson at a local hardware or home improvement store to find the one that is right for your home.

THERMOSTATS 101

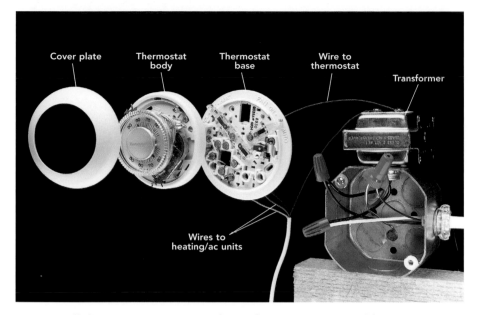

Cover plate · Thermostat body · Thermostat base · Wire to thermostat · Transformer

Wires to heating/ac units

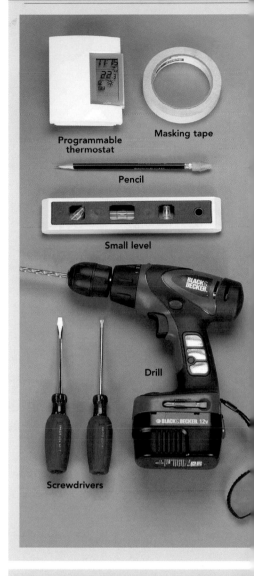

Programmable thermostat

Masking tape

Pencil

Small level

Drill

Screwdrivers

All thermostats operate on low-voltage wires powered by a trans-former, usually found attached to an electrical box near your fur-nace. The number of wires attached to the thermostat can vary from four to ten, depending on the complexity of your heating and air conditioning system. If you label the wires to identify the terminals they're attached to, installing the new thermostat will be a snap. There is very little danger of shock, because the wires you'll be touching are low-voltage.

CHEAT SHEET

Here's the common function of the screw connections you'll find in the standard thermostat controlling a forced-air furnace and central air conditioner.

- R = hot wire from transformer. Some thermostats have Rh and Rc connections if there are separate transformers for the heating and cooling units. Often, the Rh and Rc connections are joined together in the thermostat.
- C = common wire from transformer. Some thermostats don't use this connection.
- G = control for blower fan
- W = heating element
- Y = air conditioner compressor

SKILLS YOU'LL NEED

- Reading package directions
- Making wire connections (page 12)

SAFETY TIP

If your old thermostat has a vial of mercury in it, make sure to contact your local hazardous waste authorities to learn how to dispose of it safely. Mercury was used in thermostats from the 1950s to the 1970s.

DIFFICULTY LEVEL

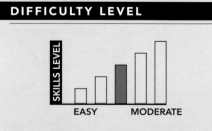

SKILLS LEVEL

EASY   MODERATE

Allow 1 to 2 hours for this project.

1 To remove the old thermostat, first switch off the power to the heating and cooling system at the main panel. Remove the cover from the old thermostat. In most cases, the cover will snap off when pulled firmly from the bottom. If it does not pull off, look for any small securing screws, and unscrew them to release the cover.

2 Next, remove the dial itself, which is held in place by a couple of small screws. You should be able to pull the dial off and expose the mounting plate beneath.

3 The mounting plate has several screws connected to wires (between three and eight wires, generally). There will also be two or three screws that hold the plate to the wall. Begin removing the plate by unscrewing these screws completely.

4 You can now pull the mounting plate away from the wall. Before you disconnect the wires, though, take a moment to label them according to the screws they're attached to on the mounting plate.

If you have a box-shaped thermostat rather than a dial-shaped one, replacing it isn't much different. You will remove the cover (A), disconnect the thermostat body (B), label and disconnect the wires (C), and remove the mounting plate from the wall (D). Then follow the directions on the following page, starting with step 6.

5 When all the wires are labeled, remove the plate completely by unscrewing all the screws that hold the wires. Take care not to let the wires fall into the wall cavity. Inspect the ends of the wires. They should be clean and free of scorching or dirt. If they aren't clean, clip off the stripped portion and then strip away ½" of insulation to expose fresh wire. Bend the stripped portion into a clockwise hook with needlenose pliers.

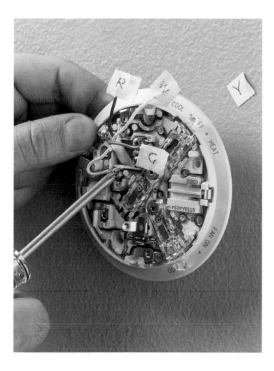

6 Now you are ready to install the new thermostat. First you'll need hang the new mounting plate. Position the plate on the wall and make certain it is level. Use a pencil to mark the new mounting holes on the wall once the plate is level.

7 Set the mounting plate aside. Using a drill, drill out the holes for the wall anchors (typically wall anchors are included with a new thermostat; use the drill bit size recommended in the instructions).

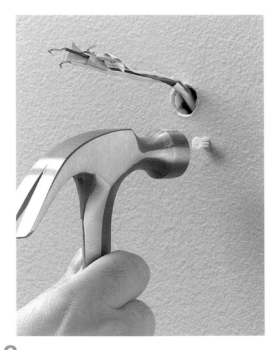

8 Press the wall anchors in the holes and push them with your fingers or gently tap them with a hammer until they are flush with the wall.

9 Reposition the wall plate over the hole, making sure that the anchors line up with the holes in the plate. Pull all of the wires through the plate. Using the screws provided with the anchors, attach the wall plate to the wall.

10 Match the labels on the wires to the corresponding screws on the new mounting plate. Connect the wires to the screw terminals on the thermostat. If the coding is different, check the instructions that came with the new thermostat to determine the wire connections for the new thermostat. There will be a table showing all the possible combinations. It's possible that one or more wires will not be used on the new thermostat. If so, tape the ends off and let them remain loose in the box.

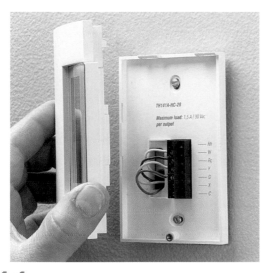

11 Install the backup batteries into the thermostat control unit, then snap the unit onto its mounting plate. Restore the power to the heating and cooling system, and test the new thermostat by turning the fan to auto and setting the temperature higher than the room temperature. The furnace fan should kick on and warm air should start to flow from the vents. If you have a cooling system, set the temperature lower than the room temperature. The air conditioner should come on and cold air should flow.

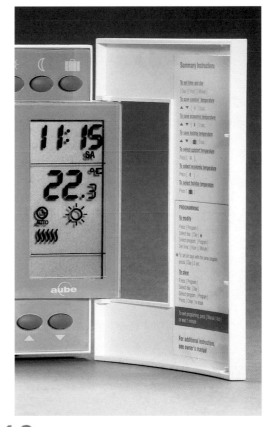

12 When you are certain that the new thermostat is working properly, follow the instructions that came with the new thermostat to program the unit to your individual needs.

Adding a Wireless Light Switch

11

Wireless switch kits are a simple and inexpensive way to add a second switch to an existing fixture.

SOMETIMES A LIGHT SWITCH IS JUST IN THE WRONG PLACE, or it would be more convenient to have two switches controlling a single fixture. Adding a second switch the conventional way generally requires hours of work and big holes in walls. (Electricians call this a "three-way" switch installation.) Fortunately, wireless switch kits are available to perform basically the same function for a fraction of the cost and effort. There is a bit of real wiring involved here, but it's not nearly as complicated as the traditional method of adding a three-way switch installation.

The kits work by replacing a conventional switch with a unit that has a built-in radio-frequency receiver that will "read" a remote device mounted within a 50 ft. radius. The kits come with a remote, battery-powered switch (it looks like a standard light switch) that you can attach to a wall with double-sided tape.

Two other similar types of wireless switch kits are also available. One allows you to control a plugged-in lamp or appliance with a remote light switch. The second type allows you to control a conventional light fixture remotely, but instead of replacing the switch, the receiver screws in below the lightbulb. This is particularly useful if you want to control a pull-chain light from a wall switch.

WIRELESS SWITCHES 101

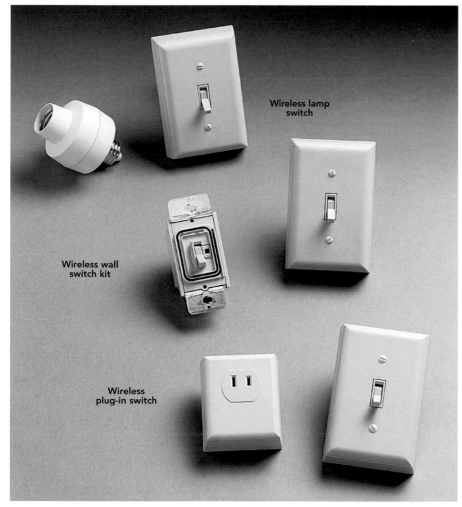

Wireless kits are available to let you switch lights on and off remotely in a variety of ways, at the switch, at the plug, or at the bulb socket.

The remote switch is a wireless transmitter that requires a battery. The transmitter switch attaches to the wall with adhesive tape or velcro strips.

TOOLS & SUPPLIES YOU'LL NEED

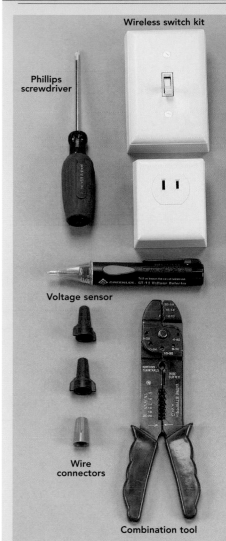

Wireless switch kit

Phillips screwdriver

Voltage sensor

Wire connectors

Combination tool

SKILLS YOU'LL NEED

- Turning off the power (page 10)
- Testing for power (page 11)
- Making wire connections (page 12)

DIFFICULTY LEVEL

SKILLS LEVEL

EASY   HARD

This is real wiring, but you should be able to finish in about 1 hour.

HOW TO REMOVE A WALL SWITCH

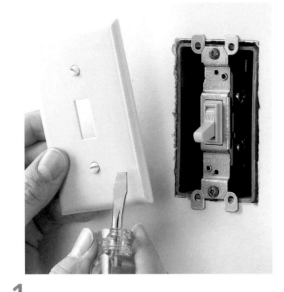

1 To remove the old switch, first shut off the power to the switch. Remove the decorative cover-plate from the switch by unscrewing the two screws that hold the plate to the switch box. Set the screws and the plate aside. With the cover-plate off, you will be able to see the switch and the electrical box it is attached to.

2 Use a voltage sensor to make sure the wires are dead. Hold your voltage sensor's probe within ½" of the wires on either side of the switch. If the sensor beeps or lights up, then the switch is still live, and you'll need to trip the correct breaker to disconnect power to the switch. If the sensor does not beep or light up, the circuit is dead and you're safe to continue.

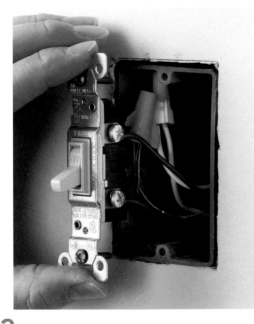

3 Remove the switch from the box by unscrewing the two long screws that hold the switch to the box at the top and the bottom. Once the screws are out, hold the top and bottom of the switch, and carefully pull the switch away from the box.

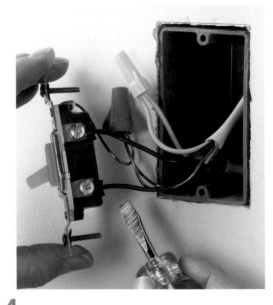

4 Remove the switch completely by disconnecting the wires. In many cases, there will also be two white wires connected with a wire connector in the box. You won't have to deal with these in your installation.

HOW TO INSTALL A WIRELESS WALL SWITCH

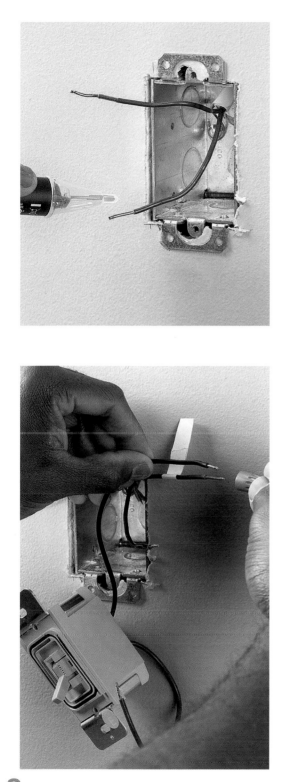

1 To install the receiver switch, you'll need to determine which wire carries current from the service panel. Bend both the wires so they are as far apart as possible. Turn the power back on temporarily. Without touching either wire, pass your voltage sensor over both. One should make your sensor beep and light up and the other won't. The one that trips your sensor carries current. Turn off the power and label that wire with a piece of tape.

3 Once the wires are firmly connected, you can attach the switch to the box. Tuck the new switch and wires neatly back into the box. Then drive the two long screws that are attached to the new switch into the two holes in the electrical box.

2 Identify the wire lead on the receiver switch marked "line" and attach it to the circuit wire you marked with tape, using a wire connector. Connect the other wire lead on the switch to the remaining circuit wire in the same way.

4 Reattach the coverplate. Then, turn the power back on at the main panel and test the switch for operation. You should be able to turn the light on and off as normal.

5 Now you can install the transmitter switch. Install the 9-volt battery in the transmitter switch. Remove the backing from the double-sided tape on the back of the switch and place the switch on a wall within 50 ft. of the receiver switch.

6 Test the operation of both switches. Each switch should successfully turn the light fixture on and off. You've just successfully created a three-way switch installation, without running any new wires.

1 You can also purchase wireless switch kits that control plug-in fixtures. Plug the receiver unit into any receptacle.

2 The unit has a receptacle on its face. Plug a lamp or any other plug-in device into the unit (this is an especially handy way to control Christmas lights).

VARIATION: WIRELESS SWITCH FOR A CEILING FIXUTURE

1 A third type of wireless switch uses a transmitter that screws into the bulb socket of the light fixture. If you need to control a light with a pull-chain switch or if you don't want to replace a wall switch as shown above, this is the best choice. Remove the lightbulb and thread the receiver into the bulb socket.

2 Screw the lightbulb into the receiver socket.

12

Fixing a Bad Receptacle

Since receptacles don't have moving parts, they don't wear out quickly, but they don't last forever. If a receptacle won't hold a plug or if it's hot to the touch or sparks when you pull a plug, it needs some attention and possibly replacement. If you have a GFCI receptacle (inset) see page 74 to 77 to replace it.

THE THING YOU'VE PROBABLY CALLED AN "OUTLET" IS MORE PROPERLY KNOWN AS AN ELECTICAL "RECEPTACLE." A receptacle that gets a lot of use will eventually wear out—you'll know this has happened if appliance plugs feel loose in the receptacle, or if a lamp flickers when the plug is jiggled. Another common problem is wires that work loose, causing the receptacle to stop working. This project will show you how to check the wire connections, then replace the receptacle if it's bad.

RECEPTACLES 101

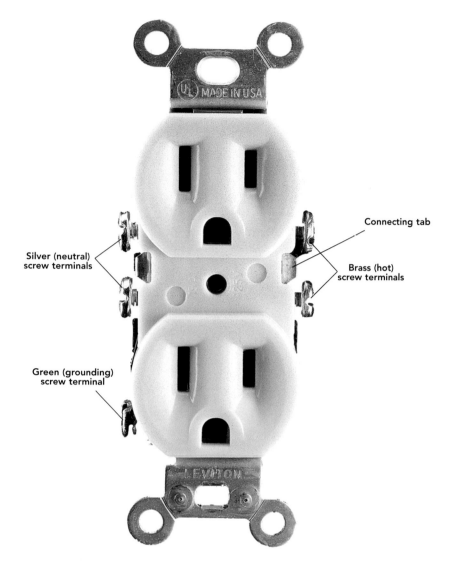

Silver (neutral) screw terminals

Connecting tab

Brass (hot) screw terminals

Green (grounding) screw terminal

Receptacles have five screws for connecting wires: two silver, two brass colored, and one green. Some installations don't use all of these screws. Disconnecting and connecting a switch is only a matter of connecting the right wires to the right screws.

TERMS YOU NEED TO KNOW

MOUNTING STRAP—the metal piece that holds the plastic body of the receptacle to the electrical box.

SCREW TERMINALS—the silver and brass-colored screws used to connect the lamp wire to the socket.

TOOLS & SUPPLIES YOU'LL NEED

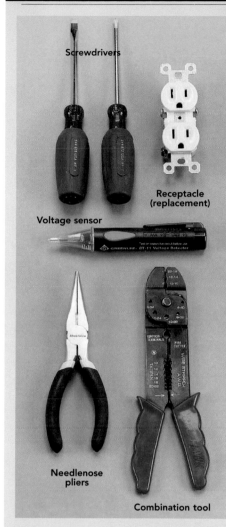

Screwdrivers

Receptacle (replacement)

Voltage sensor

Needlenose pliers

Combination tool

SKILLS YOU'LL NEED

• Turning off the power (page 10)

• Testing for power (page 11)

• Making wire connections (page 12)

DIFFICULTY LEVEL

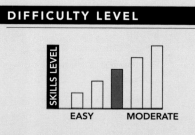

SKILLS LEVEL

EASY   MODERATE

This project takes about 1 hour.

1 Shut off the power to the switch at the main service panel. Remove the decorative coverplate from the receptacle. Set the screw and the plate aside. With the coverplate off, you will be able to see the receptacle and the electrical box it is attached to.

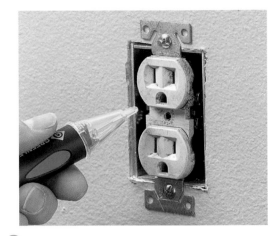

2 Use a voltage sensor to make sure that the circuit is dead. Hold your voltage sensor's probe within ½" of the wires on either side of the receptacle. If the sensor beeps or lights up, then the receptacle is still live, and you'll need to trip the correct breaker to disconnect power to the receptacle. If the sensor does not beep or light up, the receptacle is dead and you're safe to continue.

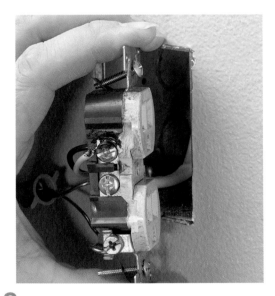

3 Remove the receptacle from the box by unscrewing the two long screws that hold the switch to the box at the top and the bottom. Once the screws are out, carefully pull the receptacle away from the box. Depending on how your receptacle has been wired, it may be connected to two colored wires and a bare grounding wire, or four colored wires and a bare wire.

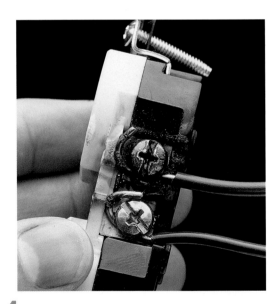

4 Inspect the screws where the wires connect to the switch. They should be tight and the connections should be clean and free of any scorch marks. If the connections were good, the problem is likely with the receptacle itself. If one of the wires is loose or if the connections are scorched, the problem is probably a loose screw causing a short circuit. You can follow the directions below to reattach the old switch or you can install a new one to be on the safe side.

5 Loosen the screw terminals and remove the circuit wires. Inspect the wires, and if they're damaged, clip them off and strip about ¾" of bare wire, using a combination tool. Check the connecting tabs on the sides of the receptacle. If they have been snapped off, you'll need to also do this on the new receptacle, using needlenose pliers

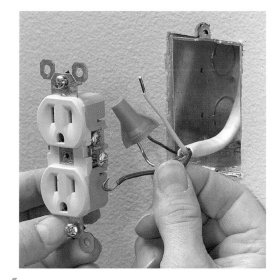

6 Use needlenose pliers to bend the stripped portions in small, clockwise hooks. Now you can connect the wires to the receptacle. Take one of the black wires and wrap the end of the wire around one of the two brass-colored screws on the side of the switch. Tighten the screw so it's snug. If there is a second black wire, wrap it around the other brass-colored screw in the same way.

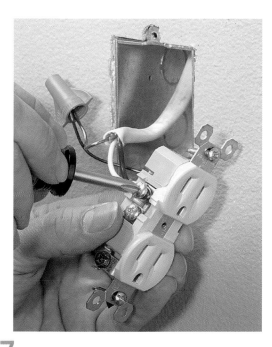

7 Now take one of the white wires and wrap the end of the wire around one of the silver screws. Tighten the screw so it's snug. Do the same for the second white wire if there is one. Connect the copper wire to the green-colored screw on the bottom of the receptacle.

8 Once the connections are made, gently tuck the wires and the receptacle in to the box so the holes at top and bottom of the receptacle align with the holes in the box. Use a screwdriver to drive the two long mounting screws that hold the receptacle to the box. Replace the cover plate. Restore the power and test your receptacle.

Childproofing Receptacles

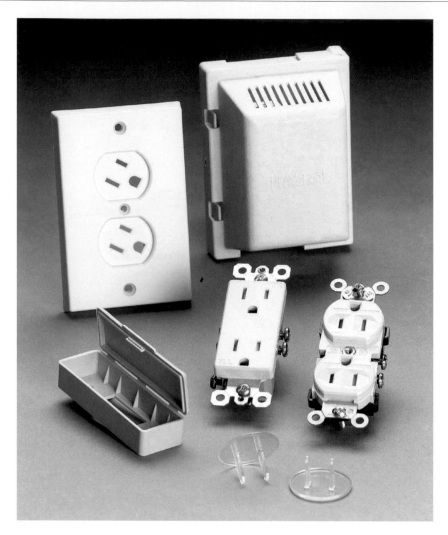

Standard receptacles present a real shock hazard to small children. Fortunately, there are many ways you can make receptacles safer without making them less convenient.

THOUSANDS OF CHILDREN ARE SHOCKED EVERY YEAR when they insert foreign objects in receptacles. Plug-in safety caps are an effective solution, but they make receptacles less convenient. Installing a tamper-resistant receptacle is an easy variation of replacing a bad receptacle (pages 64 to 65). And there are some other simple solutions that will allow you to childproof receptacles in just a few minutes.

CHILDPROOFING 101

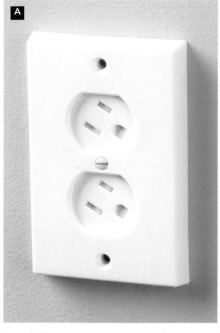

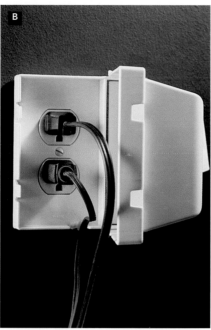

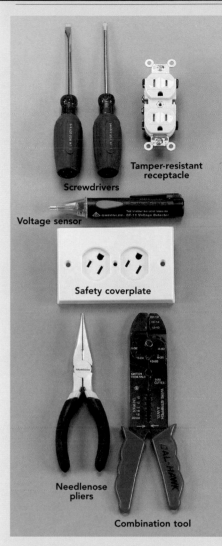
Safety coverplates (A) are designed so plugs need to be twisted before they can be fully inserted. Plug covers (B) replace standard coverplates and allow you to plug in lamps or other devices and then cover the plugs, preventing curious fingers from removing the plugs. Tamper-resistant receptacles (C) feature spring-loaded shutters that remain closed unless the two prongs of a plug enter the slots simultaneously; they won't open for a single pointed object, like a screwdriver or key. A very easy solution is plug-in inserts, which effectively block the receptacle slots completely.

SKILLS YOU'LL NEED

- Turning off the power (page 10)
- Testing for power (page 11)
- Making wire connections (page 12)

DIFFICULTY LEVEL

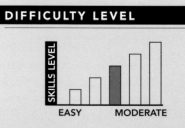

SKILLS LEVEL

EASY   MODERATE

This project will take about 1 hour.

INSTALLING A TAMPER-RESISTANT RECEPTACLE

1 Shut the power to the switch off. Remove the decorative coverplate from the receptacle by unscrewing the screw that holds the plate to the electrical box. Set the screw and the plate aside.

2 Use a voltage sensor to double-check that the circuit is dead. Hold your voltage sensor's probe within ½" of the wires on either side of the receptacle. If the sensor beeps or lights up, then the receptacle is still live, and you'll need to trip the correct breaker to disconnect power to the receptacle. If the sensor does not beep or light up, the receptacle is dead and you can proceed safely.

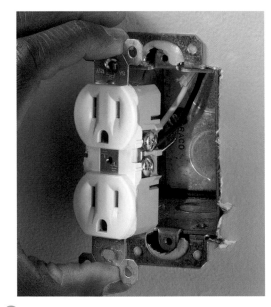

3 Remove the receptacle from the box by unscrewing the two long screws that hold the switch to the box, one at the top and another at the bottom. Once the screws are out, gently pull the receptacle away from the box. Depending on how your receptacle has been wired, there may be two colored wires and a bare wire or four colored wires and a bare wire.

4 Remove the receptacle completely by unscrewing the screws that hold the wires. Disconnect each wire by turning the screws on the sides of the receptacle just enough to free the wires.

5 Clip off the stripped ends of the wires and use your combination tool to strip away about ¾" of insulation. Then use your needlenose pliers to bend the stripped portions in small, clockwise hooks. Take one of the black wires and wrap the end of the wire around one of the two brass-colored screws on the side of the switch. Tighten the screw so it's snug. If there is a second black wire, wrap it around the other brass screw in the same way.

WHAT IF...?

What if I want a tamper-resistant GFCI receptacle?

No problem. GFCIs are available with the same shutter mechanism. Follow project #14 on page 72 to install one.

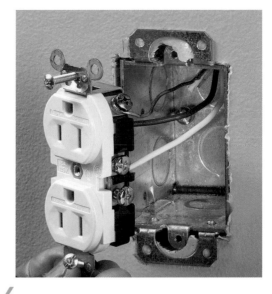

6 Now take one of the white wires and wrap the end of the wire around one of the silver screws. Tighten the screw so it's snug. Do the same for the second white wire, if there is one. Connect the copper wire to the green-colored screw on the receptacle.

7 Once the connections are made, gently tuck the wires and the receptacle in to the box so the holes at top and bottom of the receptacle align with the holes in the box. Use a screwdriver to drive the two long mounting screws that hold the receptacle to the box. Replace the coverplate. Restore the power and test your receptacle.

1 You can get much of the protection of a tamperproof outlet with a safety coverplate. Adding one takes only minutes and requires no contact with wiring. Remove the old coverplate from the receptacle by unscrewing the screw that holds the plate to the electrical box.

SAFETY TIP

Push-in slot covers cost just pennies, and can be very effective at keeping kids from poking objects into electrical receptacles. Buy several packages, and use them to plug any receptacle that your child might be tempted to play with.

2 Hold the safety coverplate over the receptacle. Use a small screwdriver to tighten the screws.

3 To plug a device in, push the slider aside and insert the plug. The shutters automatically snap over the slots when nothing is plugged in.

INSTALLING A PLUG COVER

1 Plug covers are designed to replace coverplates on receptacles where devices are plugged in more or less permanently to prevent children from unplugging them. After removing the old cover-plate, hold the plug cover's base plate over the receptacle and screw it in with a small screwdriver.

2 Plug in your lamp or other device and snap the plug cover into the new base plate. Cords should fit through the slots in the plug cover.

SAFETY TIP

Any receptacle is made safer by installing it "upside down" with the rounded grounding slot at the top. Three-prong receptacles are almost always installed with the round third prong facing down, but some experts rec-ommend wiring receptacles with the third prong on top. This is because the third prong is the grounding prong and doesn't carry any current under normal operation. In theo-ry, if something were to fall on a partially inserted plug, it would hit the harmless grounding prong and not the cur-rent-carrying slot prongs. Either way, you're wiring it right, but upside down may be slightly safer.

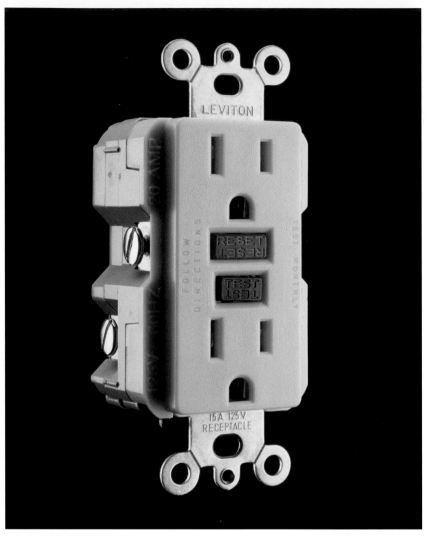

GFCI receptacles are an important protection against shocks. They work just like a normal receptacle, but they have special circuitry that helps prevent shocks. They're required by building code in all wet locations but can help improve safety anywhere.

A GROUND-FAULT CIRCUIT-INTERRUPTER RECEPTACLE (called a GFCI by pros) works just like a standard receptacle with an added feature. In the event of a short, the receptacle shuts off—"trips"—in a tiny fraction of a second. This will protect you from a dangerous shock, and this is why building codes require GFCIs in wet locations like bathrooms, kitchens, and garages.

If you need to replace a faulty receptacle in a kitchen, bathroom, or garage, replace it with a GFCI. Even if your existing receptacles work fine, you can add a measure of safety (and practice your wiring skills) by installing GFCIs. In a child's bedroom, for example, it's a good idea to install a GFCI.

GFCI 101

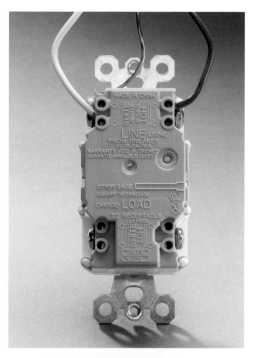

Wiring a GFCI isn't much different from wiring a standard receptacle. The main difference is that, in this installation, you'll only use one pair of the four screws, the ones labeled "line." If there were only two colored wires attached to the old receptacle, the new GFCI is attached in the same way (top photo). But If you have more than one of each color of wire connected to the old receptacle, you'll need to use a technique called pigtailing to connect the GFCI (shown in the image at left). Don't worry; it's easy and you'll see how on the next page.

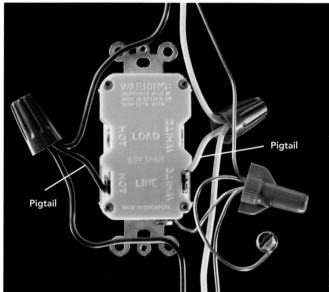

Pigtail

Pigtail

it's easy and you'll see how on the next page.

TOOLS & SUPPLIES YOU'LL NEED

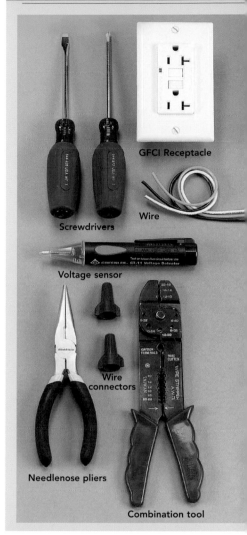

GFCI Receptacle

Wire

Screwdrivers

Voltage sensor

Wire connectors

Needlenose pliers

Combination tool

SKILLS YOU'LL NEED

- Turning off the power (page 10)
- Testing for power (page 11)
- Making wire connections (page 12)

TERMS YOU NEED TO KNOW

LOAD—In this installation, you're ignoring the screws labeled "load" and using only the ones labeled "line." The load screws literally put a load on the GFCI circuitry of the receptacle by making the GFCI protect other devices on the same circuit (so, other receptacles on the same household circuit could also trip the GFCI in the event of a short). This sounds like a good thing and it is in certain situation. But for your purposes, it will cause a lot of "nuisance" trips, where the GFCI will shut down for no apparent reason. This is why you should use the line screws only.

DIFFICULTY LEVEL

SKILLS LEVEL

EASY   HARD

This project usually takes about 1 hour.

1 Remove the decorative coverplate from the receptacle. With the coverplate off, you will be able to see the receptacle and the electrical box it is attached to.

2 Before you remove the old receptacle, use a voltage sensor to make sure the circuit is dead. Hold your voltage sensor's probe within ½" of the wires on either side of the receptacle. If the sensor beeps or lights up, then the receptacle is still live, and you'll need to trip the correct breaker to disconnect power to the receptacle. If the sensor does not beep or light up, the receptacle is dead and you can proceed safely.

3 Remove the receptacle from the box by unscrewing the long screws at the top and the bottom. Once the screws are out, gently pull the receptacle away from the box. It won't pull away easily, since the wires are still attached, so pull firmly. Depending on how your receptacle has been wired, there may be two colored wires and a bare wire or four colored wires and a bare wire.

4 Remove the receptacle completely by unscrewing the screws that hold the wires. Disconnect each wire by turning the screws on the sides of the receptacle just enough to free the wires.

5 Now you can start to connect the GFCI. To begin, count the number of wires you just disconnected from the old receptacle. You'll either have three wires—one each of white, black, and bare wires—or you'll have five—a pair of white and black wires and a single bare wire. If you've got five wires, skip to steps 6A and B. If you've got three wires, clip off the stripped ends of the wires and use your combination tool to strip away about ¾" of insulation. Then use your needlenose pliers to bend the stripped portions in small, clockwise hooks and go to step 7.

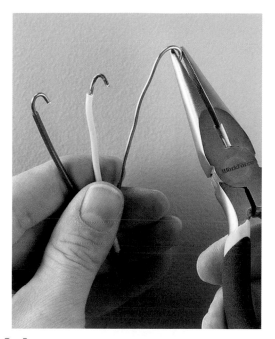

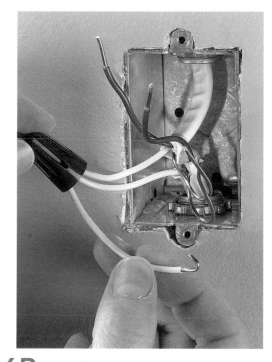

6A If you've got five wires, clip off the stripped ends of the wires and use your combination tool to strip away about ¾" of insulation. Now cut three 3" pieces of 14-gauge wire—one bare, one white, and one black. Strip about ¾" of wire from both ends and then use your needlenose pliers to make a clockwise hook at one end of each. These are your pigtails.

6B Hold the straight end of the white pigtail next to the ends of the two white wires coming from the electrical box. Slide a wire connector over the ends and twist it clockwise until the connector is snug. No bare wire should be visible. Repeat this procedure for the black wires and black pigtail, and then for the two bare wires and the bare pigtail.

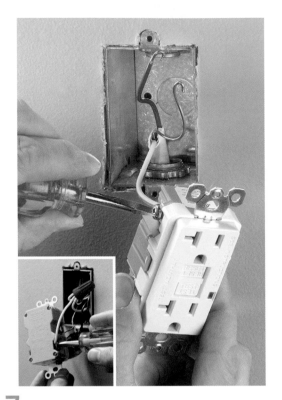

7 Connect the white wire (or the white pigtail; see inset photo) to the silver-colored screw labeled "line."

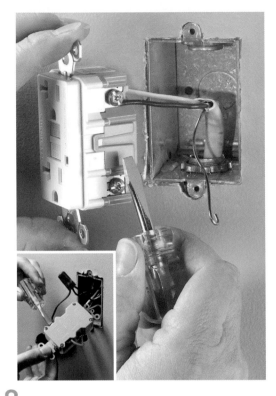

8 Connect the black wire (or the black pigtail; see inset photo) to the copper-colored screw labeled "line."

BUYING TIP

Not all GFCI receptacles are created alike. Make sure you buy one that's rated the same as the receptacle you're replacing. Many household circuits carry 15 amps of power. Receptacles for 15-amp circuits look like the one on the left. But a 20-amp circuit should have receptacles rated for 20 amps, like the one shown on the right. 20-amp receptacles have one T-shaped slot that accepts special T-shaped plugs on appliances with heavy power loads, such as window air conditioners or hot tubs.

15-amp GFCI   20-amp GFCI

9 Connect the bare wire (or the bare pigtail; see inset photo) to the green grounding screw on the bottom of the receptacle.

10 Once the connections are made, gently tuck the wires and the receptacle into the box so the holes in the top and bottom of the receptacle align with the holes in the box. Use a screwdriver to drive the two long mounting screws that hold the receptacle to the box. Replace the coverplate. If your GFCI didn't come with its own coverplate, you'll need to buy one with a square cutout to fit the GFCI.

11 Restore the power and test your receptacle. In addition to plugging something in to the receptacle, you need to test the two buttons on the face of the receptacle. Press the TEST button. The receptacle should make a clicking noise, the RESET button should pop out, and whatever you've plugged in should stop working. If this happens, the GFCI is wired correctly and working. Push RESET and the receptacle will work again.

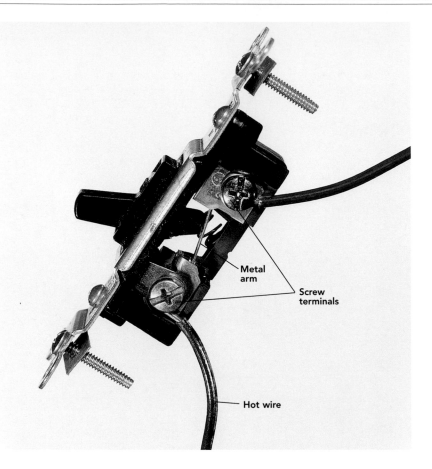

Metal arm

Screw terminals

Hot wire

Light switches have moving parts, so they do eventually wear out or stop working reliably. As shown in this cutaway, most switches have a movable metal arm that opens and closes the electrical circuit, and eventually the metal arm loses its resilience, or snaps off. You might also want to replace a switch just because you want a new look, or to install a dimmer (see page 84 to see how).

THERE ARE SEVERAL REASONS WHY YOU MIGHT NEED TO REPLACE A LIGHT SWITCH. If the switch won't stay in position (won't stay on), if it buzzes, if it gets hot, or if a breaker trips when you flip the switch, it might be time to replace the switch. And, of course, you might want to replace the switch for aesthetic reasons or to gain the added functionality of a dimmer. Dimmers not only provide greater control, but they save energy and make lightbulbs last much longer than they would at full power.

Fortunately, swapping an old switch for a new one is a very simple project. You can easily replace the standard light switch with another standard light switch using basic hand tools.

LIGHT SWITCHES 101

TERMS YOU NEED TO KNOW

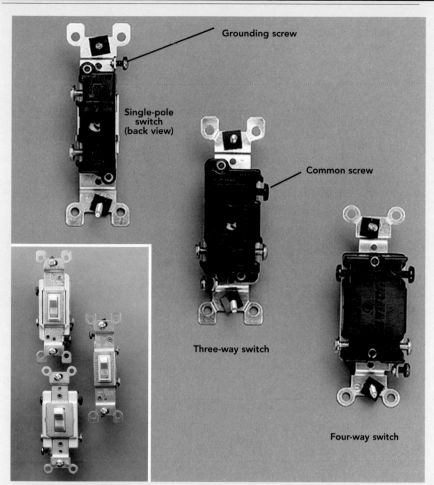

Grounding screw

Single-pole switch (back view)

Common screw

Three-way switch

Four-way switch

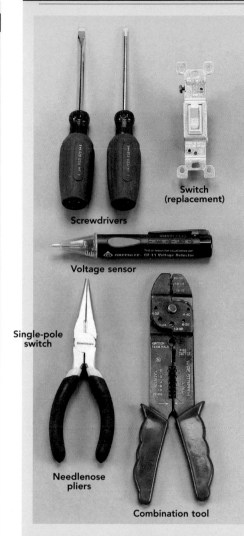

Screwdrivers

Switch (replacement)

Voltage sensor

Single-pole switch

Needlenose pliers

Combination tool

Wall switches come in three types, and it's crucial you buy the right replacement. Single-pole switches (left) are used when a light fixture is controlled from one switch location only. Notice that it has two screw terminals on the side of the switch (the screw on the metal strap used to connect the grounding wire isn't counted when you talk about circuit wires). A three-way switch (center) is used when a light fixture is controlled from two different wall locations. It has three screws on the body of the switch. One screw is known as the common terminal, the others are called travelers. A four-way switch (right) is used when a light fixture is controlled from three or more different wall locations. It has four screws on the body of the switch. Four-way switches are a little rare; you may not have any of them in your house.

When replacing a switch, remember to buy a replacement that matches the old switch, and connect the wires in the same way they were connected to the old switch.

SKILLS YOU'LL NEED

- Turning off the power (page 10)
- Testing for power (page 11)
- Making wire connections (page 12)

DIFFICULTY LEVEL

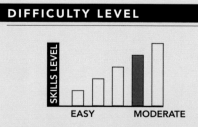

SKILLS LEVEL

EASY   MODERATE

Allow about 1 hour for this project.

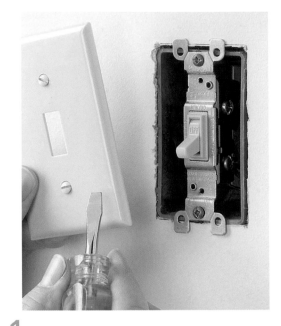

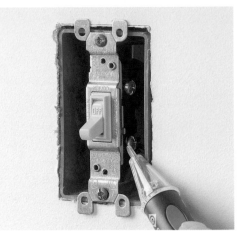

1 First shut off the power to the switch. Remove the decorative coverplate from the switch by unscrewing the two screws that hold the plate to the switch box. Set the screws and the plate aside. With the coverplate off, you will be able to see the switch and the electrical box it is attached to.

2 Use a voltage sensor to make sure the circuit is dead. Hold the sensor's probe within ½" of the wires on either side of the switch. If the sensor beeps or lights up, then the switch is still live, and you'll need to trip the correct breaker to disconnect power to the switch. If the sensor does not beep or light up, the circuit is dead and you're safe to continue.

3 Remove the switch from the box by unscrewing the two long screws that hold the switch to the box, one at the top, the other at the bottom. Once the screws are free, gently pull the switch away from the box.

4 Inspect the screw connections. They should be tight and free of any scorch marks. If one of the connections is loose or scorched, the problem is probably a loose screw causing a short circuit. Reattach the wires, reassemble the switch and coverplate, and see if the switch works. If this isn't the problem, continue to the next step.

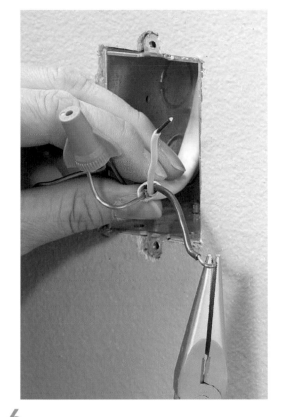

5 Loosen all the screw connections and detach the switch from the wires. (If there are three or four colored wires attached to the switch instead of just two, see the "WHAT IF" variation on the next page.) In many cases, there will also be two white wires connected with a wire connector in the box. You won't have to deal with these in your installation. Take the old switch to a hardware store or home center and purchase an identical replacement.

6 Before you begin to wire your new switch, clip of the ends of the wires and use your combination tool to strip away about ¾"of insulation. Then use your needlenose pliers to bend the stripped portion in a small clockwise hook.

WHAT IF...?

What if there is a white wire connected to the switch?

In certain installations, a switch is connected with one black wire and one white wire. (The pros call this installation a "switch loop.") If the electrician did a good job, the end of the white wire should have black tape, indicating that it carries current. Treat it just like a black wire when you install your new switch. If there is no tape on the end of the white wire, wrap a bit of electrical tape on the end. The next person who works on the circuit will thank you.

WHAT IF...?

What if there are more than two colored wires connected to the switch? If this is the case, you're dealing with a three-way switch (if there are three colored wires) or a four-way switch (if there are four colored wires). Before removing a three- or four-way switch, use masking tape to label the wires to identify which screw terminals they are attached to.

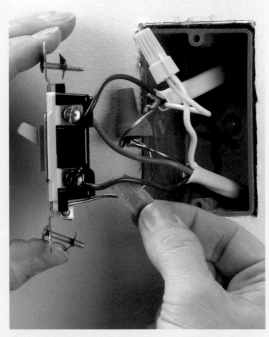

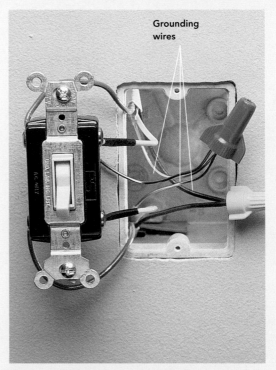

Grounding wires

For a three-way switch, one screw terminal is labeled "common," and is almost always darker in color than the other two. Make sure the wire that was attached to the common screw terminal on the old switch is connected to the common screw terminal on the new switch. The other two wires aren't critical; they can be attached to either of the remaining screw terminals.

Four-way switches are a little trickier. In most cases, you'll be attaching the pair of wires attached to the top two screw terminals on the old switch to the same screws on the new switch. Then you'll attach the other pair of wires to the bottom pair of screws. Some manufacturers, though, use a different pairing system, with one screw terminal pair on the right side of the switch, the other on the left. A good way to avoid problems is by buying a replacement made by the same manufacturer that made the old switch.

7 Position the switch so the ON/OFF markings read correctly. Take one of the colored circuit wires and wrap the end of the wire clockwise around one of the two screw terminals on the side of the switch. Tighten the screw so it's snug. Wrap the second colored wire around the other screw in the same way. If there was a bare copper wire connected to the old switch, connect it to the green-colored screw on the switch in the same way you connected the two black wires. (If you're installing a three-way or four-way, see the information on the opposite page.) Then connect the rest of the wires as described above. The other two screws are interchangeable, so it doesn't matter which of the remaining colored wires connects to which screw.

8 Check to make sure the white circuit wires (they're called the neutrals) are snugly connected. If not, then use a wire nut to join them.

9 Once the connections are made, gently tuck the wires and the switch into the box so the holes in the top and bottom of the switch align with the holes in the box. Use a screwdriver to drive the two long mounting screws that hold the switch to the box. Replace the coverplate. Restore the power and test your switch.

16

Installing a Dimmer

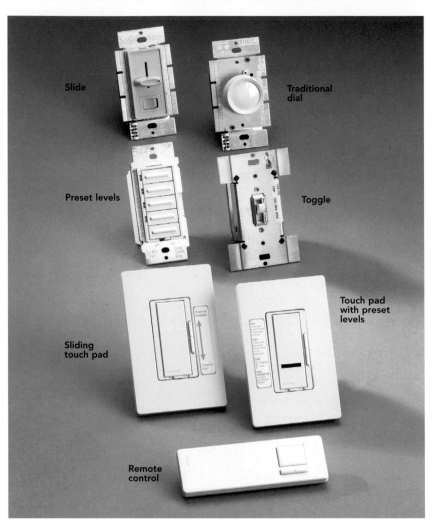

Slide

Traditional dial

Preset levels

Toggle

Sliding touch pad

Touch pad with preset levels

Remote control

Dimmers not only allow you to fine-tune the amount of light in a room, but also they save energy and extend lightbulb life. There is a wide variety of dimmer switches available to replace almost any standard ON/OFF switch. Whether you flip, turn, slide, or touch them, they all work the same. The one exception is an automatic dimmer, which has an electronic sensor that adjusts the light fixture to compensate for the changing levels of natural light. An automatic dimmer also can be operated manually.

DIMMER SWITCHES ARE SIMPLY LIGHT SWITCHES that allow you to control the intensity of light that comes from a fixture. The control may be a dial, a touch pad, a slider, or a faux-toggle switch, but they all function in basically the same way.

Installing a dimmer is no more difficult than installing a light switch. The only possible obstacles are the size of the electrical box and the type of light in the fixture. In some older homes, the metal box that contains the old switch may not be large enough for a dimmer. If the fixture uses fluorescent lightbulbs, you will not be able to use a standard dimmer.

DIMMER SWITCHES 101

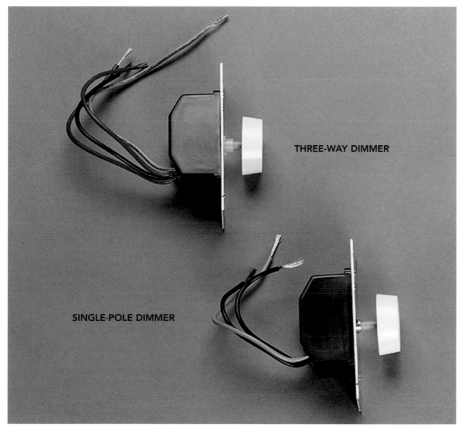

THREE-WAY DIMMER

SINGLE-POLE DIMMER

Unlike standard light switches, dimmers are connected to the household electrical wires by short lengths of wire called "leads." Leads come pre-attached to the dimmer. You attach them to the household wiring with wire connectors. Single-pole dimmers have two wire leads (plus a green grounding lead). Use this type for switches where the light fixture is controlled from a single wall location. Three-way dimmers have three black and red wire leads, and are used when a light fixture is controlled from two wall locations.

TERMS YOU NEED TO KNOW

COMMON WIRE—On a three-way wall switch or dimmer, one of the screw terminals or wire leads is designated as "common." Depending on where the switch is in the circuit, the common wire receives electrical current from the power source, or sends current to the light fixture. The common screw terminal or wire lead is the one that is a different color from the other two screws or wire leads.

TRAVELER WIRE—On three way switches and dimmers, the travelers are the two wires other than the common (see above). The traveler wires run between the two switches, providing alternative paths for electrical current.

TOOLS & SUPPLIES YOU'LL NEED

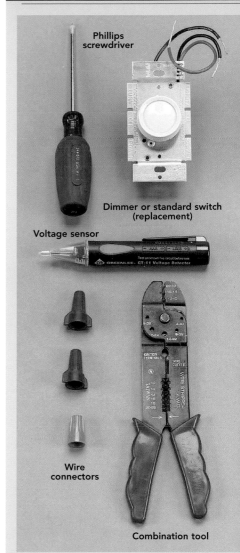

Phillips screwdriver

Dimmer or standard switch (replacement)

Voltage sensor

Wire connectors

Combination tool

SKILLS YOU'LL NEED

- Turning off the power (page 10)
- Testing for power (page 11)
- Making wire connections (page 12)

DIFFICULTY LEVEL

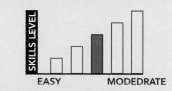

SKILLS LEVEL

EASY   MODEDRATE

Allow 1 to 2 hours for this job.

HOW TO INSTALL A DIMMER SWITCH

1 First shut off the power to the switch. Remove the decorative coverplate from the switch by unscrewing the two screws that hold the plate to the switch box. Set the screws and the plate aside. With the coverplate off, you will be able to see the switch and the electrical box it is attached to.

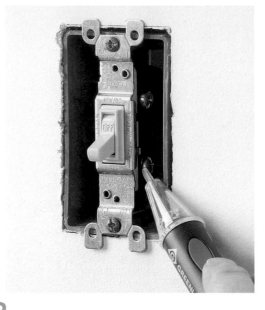

2 Use a voltage sensor to make sure that the circuit is dead. Hold your voltage sensor's probe within ½" of the wires on either side of the switch. If the sensor beeps or lights up, then the switch is still live, and you'll need to trip the correct breaker to disconnect power to the switch. If the sensor does not beep or light up, the circuit is dead and you are safe to continue.

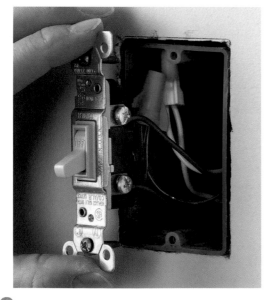

3 Remove the switch from the box by unscrewing the two long screws that hold it. One is at the top and another at the bottom. Once the screws are out, hold the top and bottom of the switch, and gently pull the switch away from the box.

WHAT IF...?

What if my electrical box seems too small to hold the dimmer switch? Dimmer switches have much bigger bodies than standard switches, and they are connected with twist wire connectors rather than screw terminal connections. This means that the electrical box might be too small to hold the switch and the connections. If so, don't try to force the switch into the box. Instead, see the Here's How feature on page 89.

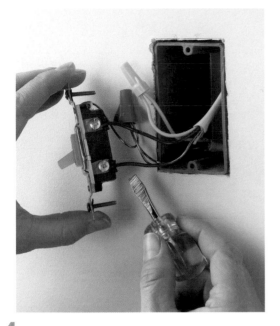

4 Remove the switch completely by unscrewing the screws that hold the wires. There may be as many as four wires connected to the switch: black, white, bare copper, and red. Disconnect each one by turning the screws on the sides of the switch just enough to free the wires. In many cases, there will also be two white wires connected with a wire connector in the box. You won't have to deal with these in your installation.

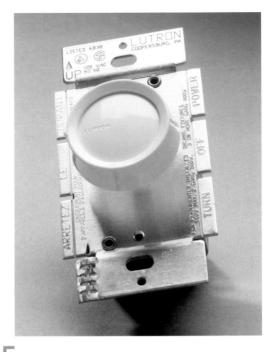

5 Buy a dimmer suited for your replacement. Choose a single-pole or three-way dimmer, as needed. Second, buy a dimmer rated for the maximum wattage of all light fixtures the switch will serve. For example, if the standard light switch you are replacing controls three recessed 60-watt lights, then the dimmer switch should be rated for 180 watts ($60 \times 3 = 180$).

WHAT IF...?

What if you find four colored wires attached to your switch?

This is a four-way switch, a type of switch used to control light fixtures from three or more different switch locations. A four-way switch can't be replaced with a dimmer, so if you run into this situation, you'll need to reassemble the switch. However, four-way switch installations are always installed in conjunction with three-way switches in the other switch locations. You will be able to replace one of the three-way switches at a different wall location with a three-way dimmer switch.

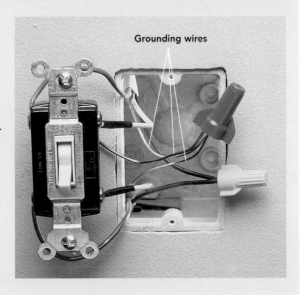

Grounding wires

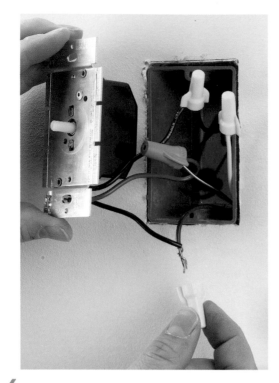

6 The dimmer will have two black wires, called leads, coming out of the dimmer's plastic body. The leads, like the two black wires coming out of the wall, are interchangeable, so you can't mix them up. Place the stripped end of one of the black leads and the end of one of the existing black wires into a wire connector (the dimmer will come with twist-on wire connectors). Twist the wire connector clockwise until it is tight. Hold the wires and tug gently on the connector to ensure that it is tight. Connect the other lead to the other wire from the wall in the same way. (If you are installing a three-way dimmer, see "WHAT IF…?" at right.)

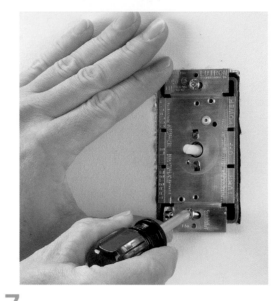

7 Once the wires are firmly connected, you can attach the switch to the box. Tuck the new switch and wires neatly back into the box. Then drive the two long screws that are attached to the new switch into the two holes in the electrical box. These screws are typically long, so an electric screwdriver is handy. Reattach the coverplate. Then, turn the power back on at the main panel and test the switch for operation.

WHAT IF…?

If you're installing a three-way dimmer, attach the wire lead identified as the common to the circuit wire you tagged as the common in step 4. Now attach the other two wire leads to the other two colored circuit wires, using wire connectors. These wires, called the travelers, are interchangeable. It doesn't make any difference which of the two remaining circuit wires they get attached to.

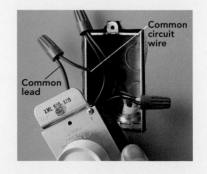

Common circuit wire

Common lead

Dimmer switches have larger bodies than traditional toggle switches, so you may find that the existing electrical box is too small to comfortably hold the new dimmer switch. Shallow, 2"-deep electrical boxes will not easily accommodate dimmer switches, especially if there are more than one set of wires inside the electrical box. If you purchase a dimmer and can't seem to get it to fit, don't force it. Dimmers produce more heat than standard switches, and it is a potential fire hazard to crowd the electrical box. You may be able to find a dimmer with a smaller body that will fit. Or, you can install a new, larger wall box.

Installing a new wall box is a somewhat advanced project, so you may want to hire a professional to do this work. But if you're up to the task, you can do it yourself by following the directions below. Allow yourself a full afternoon for this graduate school project.

1 Remove the old switch, following steps 1 through 5 on pages 86 and 87. To remove the old box, identify the location of the nails holding the electrical box to the wall studs. Use a reciprocating saw or jigsaw equipped with a metal-cutting blade to cut through the nails holding the box.

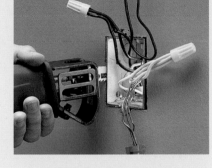

2 Bind the cable ends together and attach them to strings so they don't fall into the wall cavity when the old box is removed. Disconnect the cable clamps and slide the old box out.

3 Feed the cable into the new box, tighten the cable clamps, and secure the box in the opening. The retrofit box shown here uses bracket arms that are inserted into the sides of the box, then bent around the front edges to secure the box in the opening. Other styles of retrofit boxes have other means of attachment. Attach the new dimmer, following steps 6 and 7 on the preceding page.

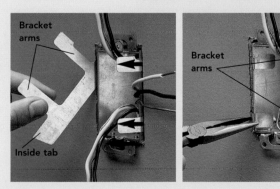

Bracket arms

Inside tab

Bracket arms

Installing a Timer Switch

17

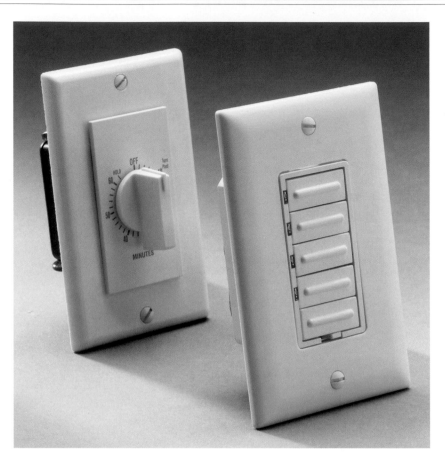

There are two common types of timer switch. Dial-type timers are commonly used to control bathroom vents and outdoor lights. To turn on the light and set the timer, simply twist the dial to the desired setting. When the dial winds down, the light or fan goes off. Push-button timers are commonly used to control lights. They have three or four switches, each with a preset time setting.

TIMER SWITCHES ARE SIMPLY SWITCHES THAT TURN ON OR OFF after a determined amount of time. This is useful for controlling some types of exterior lights and for controlling bathroom vent fans. With outdoor lights, you can use a timer to turn on landscape and security lighting at preset times. In the bathroom, the timer can vastly increase the efficacy of your vent fan by making sure it runs long enough to completely evacuate moist air. You can also use push-button-type timer switches to control room lights, thus assuring that no light is left burning indefinitely.

Installing a timer is no more difficult than installing a light switch. As with dimmers, the size of the box holding the switch in the wall is a consideration. In some older homes, the metal box that contains the old switch may not be large enough for a timer. If so, see page 89 for information on changing the box.

TIMER SWITCHES 101

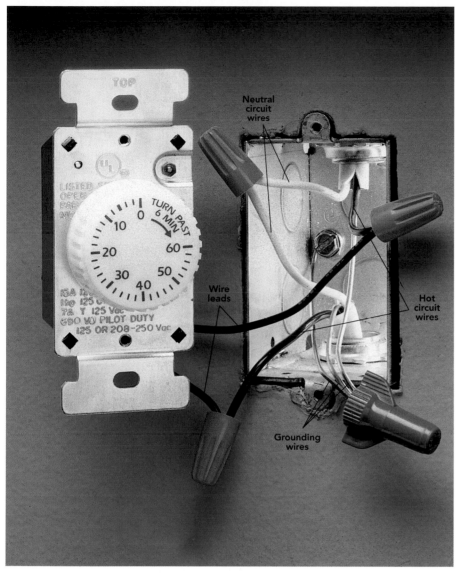

Unlike standard light switches and like dimmers, most timers are connected to the household electrical wires by short lengths of wire called leads. Leads come preattached to the timer. You attach them to the household wiring with wire connectors.

TERMS YOU NEED TO KNOW

LEADS—The preattached black wires attached to a timer switch.

GROUNDING WIRES—The bare copper circuit wires in an electrical box.

TOOLS & SUPPLIES YOU'LL NEED

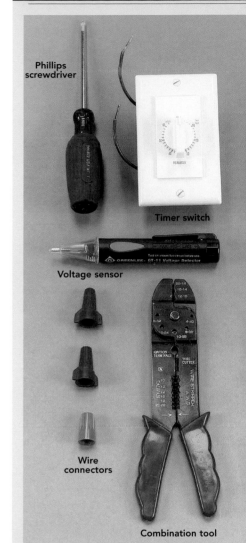

SKILLS YOU'LL NEED

• Turning off the power (page 10)

• Testing for power (page 11)

• Making wire connections (page 12)

DIFFICULTY LEVEL

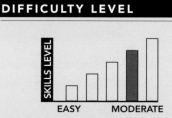

This project takes about 1 hour.

HOW TO INSTALL A TIMER SWITCH

1 First shut off the power to the switch. Remove the decorative coverplate from the switch by unscrewing the two screws that hold the plate to the switch box. Set the screws and the plate aside.

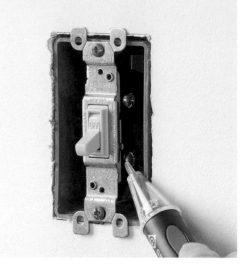

2 Use a voltage sensor to make sure the circuit is dead. Hold your voltage sensor's probe within ½" of the wires on either side of the switch. If the sensor beeps or lights up, then the switch is still live, and you'll need to trip the correct breaker to disconnect power to the switch. If the sensor does not beep or light up, the circuit is dead and you're safe to continue.

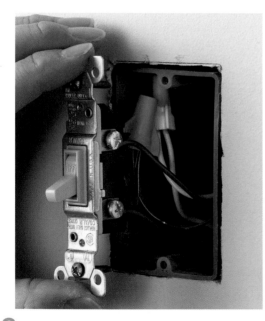

3 Remove the switch from the box by unscrewing the two long screws that hold the switch to the box at the top and at the bottom. Once the screws are out, hold the top and bottom of the switch, and carefully pull the switch away from the box.

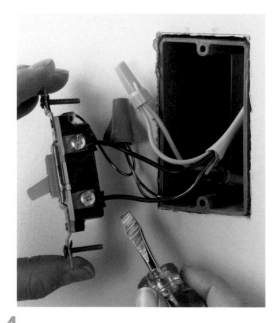

4 Remove the switch completely by unscrewing the screws that hold the two wires to the switch. In most cases, there will also be two white wires connected with a wire connector in the box. You won't have to deal with these in your installation.

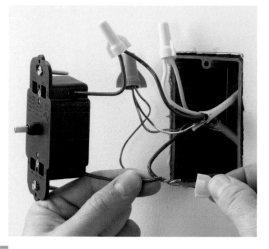

5 The timer will have two black wires, called leads, coming out of the timer's plastic body. The leads, like the two black wires coming out of the wall, are interchangeable, so you can't mix them up. Place the stripped end of one of the black leads and the end of one of the existing black wires into a wire connector (the dimmer will come with twist-on wire connectors). Twist the wire connector clockwise until it is tight. Hold the wires and tug gently on the connector to ensure that it is tight. Connect the other lead to the other wire from the wall in the same way.

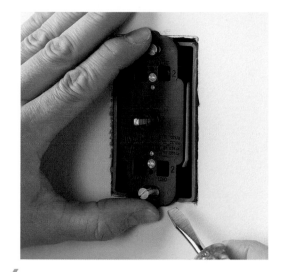

6 Once the wires are firmly connected, you can attach the switch to the box. Tuck the new timer switch and wires neatly back into the box. Then drive the two long screws that are attached to the new switch into the two holes in the electrical box. These screws are typically long, so an electric screwdriver is handy. Pull the dial off the timer so the coverplate will fit over it. Reattach the coverplate and push the dial back onto the timer stem. Then, turn the power back on at the main panel and test the switch.

WHAT IF...?

What if there's a light switch right next to the fan switch?

This is a common arrangement. You might even find a group of three switches together. Behind the single coverplate, you'll find one large electrical box, called a "double-gang" box if there are two switches, that contains all the connections. This won't affect your installation except in one way: the coverplate. The coverplate that comes with your timer will be for a single switch. You'll need to buy a double-gang coverplate with a cutout for your timer (a small hole in the center) and one for a standard light switch.

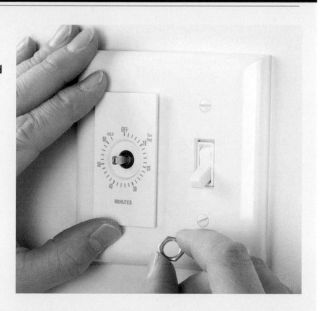

18

Installing Low-voltage Cable Lights

Low-voltage cable lights are a flexible and attractive way to update a lighting design. It doesn't take more than a couple of hours to replace a standard ceiling fixture with a low-voltage cable system.

LOW-VOLTAGE CABLE LIGHTS are one of the newest developments in lighting. They offer many of the advantages of track lighting, but are even easier to install and often less expensive. The light fixtures can be moved along the cable and aimed individually to achieve the desired mood or task lighting, making them an ideal replacement for a central fixture that casts too many shadows. Replacing an old ceiling-mounted light fixture with a low-voltage cable light is a fairly simple project.

Before you begin, it's important to spend some time planning the location of the cables and lights. Investigate the area you would like to light. You can use a yardstick or tape measure to identify the length, the placement of cables, and the number of lights that you will need to achieve the effect you're looking for.

LOW-VOLTAGE LIGHTS 101

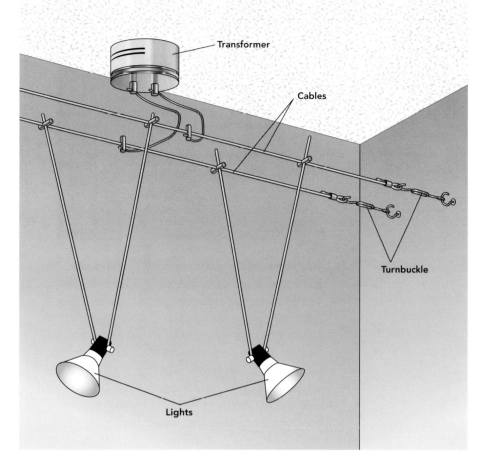

Transformer

Cables

Turnbuckle

Lights

Low-voltage cable lights run off a transformer that reduces 120-volt current to 12 volts. Current runs along the cables to the hanging light fixtures. This means that there is low risk of electrical shock from the cables as long as the location is dry. The low-voltage system includes a transformer, cables, and lights. The cables are secured in the walls using a turnbuckle system that allows you to pull the wires between the walls and tighten.

TERMS YOU NEED TO KNOW

LOW-VOLTAGE LIGHTING—For indoor lighting purposes, low voltage means 12 volts or, rarely, 24 volts. Normal voltage is 120 volts.

TRANSFORMER—An electrical device that steps up voltage and steps down current proportionally (or vice versa). In lighting applications, transformers take 120 volts down to 12.

HALOGEN—Low-voltage systems use small halogen bulbs. Halogen bulbs work like regular incandescent lightbulbs, except the bulbs are filled with halogen gas, making the bulbs burn brighter at a lower voltage.

TOOLS & SUPPLIES YOU'LL NEED

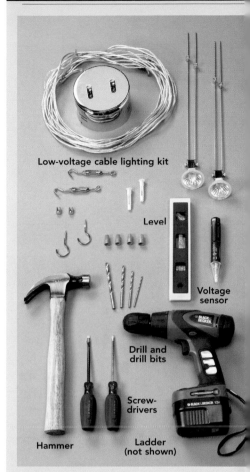

Low-voltage cable lighting kit

Level

Voltage sensor

Drill and drill bits

Screw-drivers

Hammer

Ladder (not shown)

SKILLS YOU'LL NEED

- Turning off power (page 10)
- Testing for power (page 11)
- Making wire connections (page 12)
- Light carpentry tool skills

DIFFICULTY LEVEL

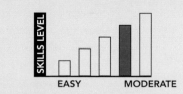

SKILLS LEVEL

EASY   MODERATE

This job takes about two hours, and is easier with two people.

1 Locate the circuit breaker that controls the existing ceiling-mounted light that you are working on, and switch that breaker into the OFF position. Close the cover of the breaker or fuse cabinet.

2 Remove the globe (many are held in place by a decorative nut in the center), and remove the lightbulbs from the fixture. Detach the old light from the ceiling electrical box. Most traditional fixtures use two long screws to secure the fixture base to the metal electrical box in the ceiling. Have a helper hold the fixture with one hand so it doesn't fall, while you use a screwdriver to remove the two screws. Gently pull the light straight down, exposing the wiring that powers the fixture.

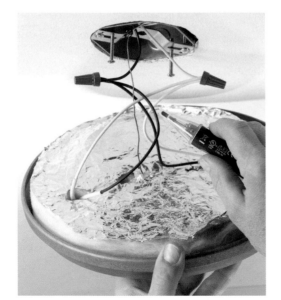

3 Before you touch the wires that feed the existing light, use a voltage sensor to verify that the circuit is now dead. Insert the sensor's probe into the electrical box and hold the probe within ½" of the black wires inside. If the sensor beeps or lights up, then the circuit is still live, and you'll need to trip the correct breaker to disconnect power to the fixture. If the sensor does not beep or light up, the circuit is dead and you're safe to continue.

4 Now remove the fixture by disconnecting the wires. Use your hands to unscrew the wire connectors by turning them counterclockwise. After removing the wire connectors, pull the fixture completely away from the box (you can recycle it or save it). If you need to stop working and restore the power, first separate the wires coming from the ceiling box and cap them each with a wire connector.

5 Plan a path for the parallel cables. The path should pass under (within a foot or so, at least) of the old fixture. Installation of the wall-anchoring system varies somewhat by manufacturer, so read and follow the specific instructions for your kit. The simplest systems use hooks and turnbuckles to tension the cables. To install, mark holes 6 to 10" apart on opposite walls at the ends of the planned cable runs.

6 Unless you know your holes go into the studs behind the walls, you'll need to anchor the hooks in the drywall with hollow wall anchors. These are simply plastic tubes that ensure the hooks will be secure in the walls. Most kits include wall anchors appropriate for the supplied hooks. Use a drill and a ¼" drill bit to make holes on your marks. Tap a plastic wall anchor into the hole with a hammer so the anchor's top is nearly level with the surface. Do this for each of the holes unless you know the hole goes into a stud.

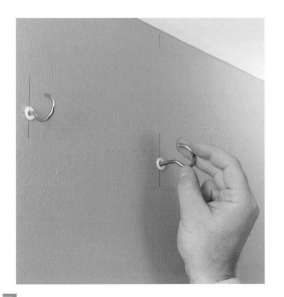

7 Now you can screw the hooks into the anchors. Screw the hooks in by hand. When they become too difficult to turn, use a pair of pliers to turn the hooks until all the threads have disappeared into the anchors.

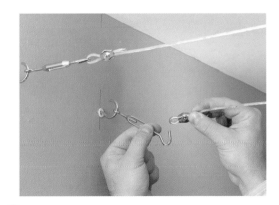

8 Measure the distance between opposite hooks, and then cut two lengths of the supplied cable to that length plus an extra 12". Use your lineman's pliers to cut the cable. Follow the manufacturer's instructions for attaching a loop to one end of each cable and a turnbuckle to the other. Then, place the loop of a cable on one hook and the turnbuckle on the opposite wall's hook. Tighten the turnbuckle to take up the slack until the cable is tight. Install the other cable in the same way. Cut away any extra cable for a clean look.

9 Make sure the power is off to the wires in the electrical box before you touch the wires or begin to install the transformer. Install the transformer crossbar to the electrical box using the two screws provided with the fixture.

10 Have a helper hold the transformer or rest it on top of a ladder while you make the electrical connections. Place the stripped end of one of the black wires from the transformer and the end of one of the black wires coming from the ceiling into a wire connector (supplied with the lighting kit). Twist the wire connector clockwise until it is tight. Connect the white wire from the transformer to the white wire coming from the electrical box. Connect the bare copper wire from the transformer to the bare copper wire coming from the electrical box.

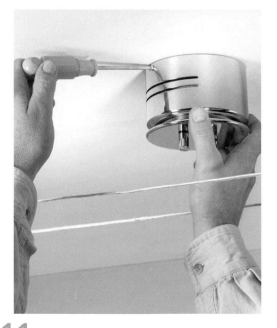

11 Connect the transformer and its decorative cover to the crossbar you installed in step 9.

HERE'S HOW

Here's how to purchase the right cable light kit. Aside from purchasing a kit that looks right for your space, you'll need one with the appropriate transformer. This project shows a "hard-wired" transformer—one that's connected directly to the household wiring. Some inexpensive kits use plug-in transformers that connect to a regular wall receptacle. They work fine, but they don't look as polished. You'll also need a transformer that supplies the right amount of power in watts. You can figure out the maximum number of watts simply by looking on the sides of the sockets of the old fixture. It should have a rating for maximum watts. Multiply this number by the number of bulb sockets. You can use a transformer that has up to this many watts.

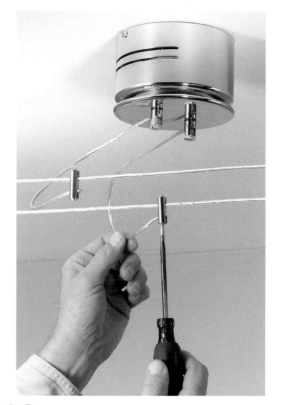

12 Now you can begin to connect the transformer to the two parallel cables you already installed. The transformer has two screw terminals somewhere on its cover. Cut two lengths of the supplied cable to reach from the screw terminals to the parallel cables. Insert one end of the cable into the screw terminal on the transformer and tighten the screw until you feel its tip pierce the insulation. Connect the other lead to the transformer in the same way.

14 At this point, it's a good idea to restore power and turn the light switch on. 12 volts won't hurt you (if you can even feel it) and it's easier to adjust the lights when they're on. The hardware used to connect the fixtures to the cables varies considerably from manufacturer to manufacturer, but most rely on some sort of setscrew to pierce each cable's insulation so current can flow to the lightbulbs. The key is to get those screws (which are often small) tight. A small, short screwdriver is very helpful.

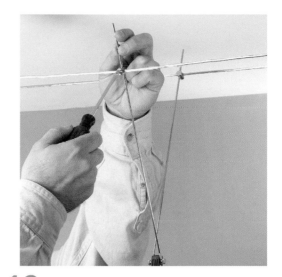

13 Using the connector supplied with the kit, connect the other end of one of the short cables to one of the two parallel cables. The key is to make sure all the screws are tight enough so their tips pierce the cable's insulation and provide a good electrical connection. Connect the other short cable to the other parallel cable in the same way.

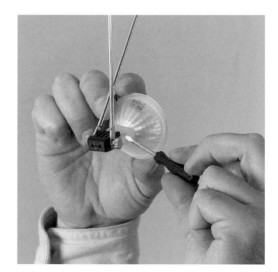

15 Once the fixtures are connected, install and adjust the bulbs so they're aimed as you like. The bulbs have two short prongs coming out of their bases. These provide the electrical connection. Typically, the prongs slide into two holes in the fixtures base and are secured by two small screws. Tightening these can be tricky. Use a small screwdriver and don't overtighten the screws. Get them just tight enough to hold the bulbs.

19

Replacing a Ceiling-mounted Fixture

Installing a new ceiling fixture can provide more light to a space, not to mention an aesthetic lift. It's one of the easiest upgrades you can do.

CEILING FIXTURES DON'T HAVE ANY MOVING PARTS and their wiring is very simple, so, other than changing bulbs, you're likely to get decades of trouble-free service from a fixture. This sounds like a good thing, but it also means that the fixture probably won't fail and give you an excuse to update a room's look with a new one. Fortunately, you can don't need an excuse. Upgrading a fixture is easy and can make a dramatic impact on a room. You can substantially increase the light in a room by replacing a globe-style fixture by one with separate spot lights, or you can simply install a new fixture that matches the room's décor.

CEILING FIXTURES 101

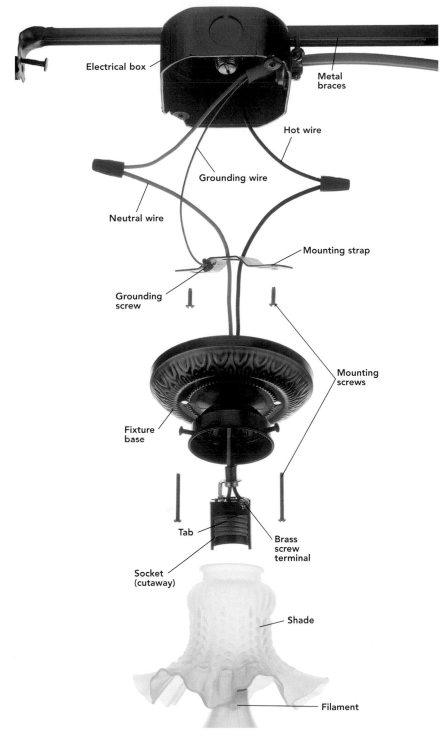

Electrical box

Metal braces

Hot wire

Grounding wire

Neutral wire

Mounting strap

Grounding screw

Mounting screws

Fixture base

Tab

Brass screw terminal

Socket (cutaway)

Shade

Filament

No matter what a ceiling light fixture looks like on the outside, they all attach in basically the same way. An electrical box in the ceiling is fitted with a mounting strap, which holds the fixture in place. The bare wire from the ceiling typically connects to the mounting strap. The two wires coming from the fixture connect to the black and white wires from the ceiling.

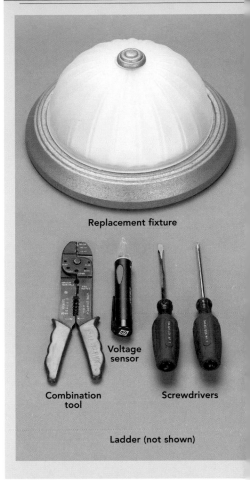

Replacement fixture

Combination tool

Voltage sensor

Screwdrivers

Ladder (not shown)

SKILLS YOU'LL NEED

- Turning off the power (page 10)
- Testing for power (page 11)
- Making wire connections (page 12)

DIFFICULTY LEVEL

SKILLS LEVEL

EASY   MODERATE

This project should take you 2 hours or less, and will be easier if you have a helper.

HOW TO REPLACE A CEILING-MOUNTED LIGHT FIXTURE

1 Begin by turning off the power to the fixture. Remove the globe by unthreading the globe (turning it counterclockwise) or by loosening the three screws that pinch the globe in place (the screws usually go through a collar around the base of the globe). Next, remove the lightbulbs from the fixture.

HERE'S HOW

Here's how to remove the shade. Most are secure in the center by a decorative nut. You can probably unscrew it by hand (hold on to the shade or have a helper support it). If it's stuck, try a pliers.

2 Detach the old light from the ceiling electrical box. Most traditional fixtures use two long screws to secure the fixture base to the metal electrical box in the ceiling. Have a helper hold the fixture with one hand so it doesn't fall, while you use a screwdriver to remove the two screws. Gently pull the light straight down, exposing the wiring that powers the fixture.

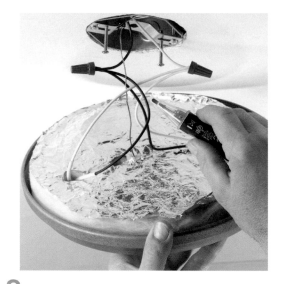

3 Before you touch the wires that feed the existing light, use a voltage sensor to verify that the circuit is now dead. With the fixture's switch in the ON position, insert the sensor's probe into the electrical box and hold the probe within ½" of the black wires inside. If the sensor beeps or lights up, then the circuit is still live, and you'll need to trip the correct breaker to disconnect power to the fixture. If the sensor does not beep or light up, the circuit is dead and you can proceed safely.

4 Once you have verified that the power to the light is off at the main panel, remove the fixture by disconnecting the wires. Use your hands to unscrew the wire connectors by turning them counterclockwise. After removing the wire connectors, pull the fixture completely away from the box (you can recycle it or save it). If you need to stop working and restore the power, first separate the wires coming from the ceiling box and cap them each with a wire connector.

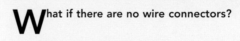

WHAT IF...?

What if there are no wire connectors?

If the fixture is small, the wires from the box may be connected directly to the fixture. To disconnect them, simply loosen the screws enough to free the wires.

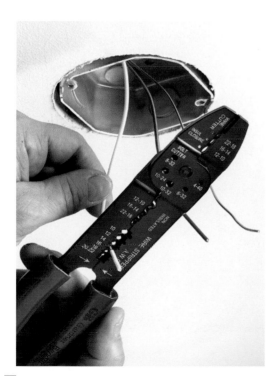

5 Before you install the new fixture, check the ends of the wires coming from the ceiling electrical box. They should be clean and free of nicks or scorch marks. If they're dirty or worn, clip off the stripped portion with your combination tool. Then, strip away about ¾" of insulation from the end of each wire.

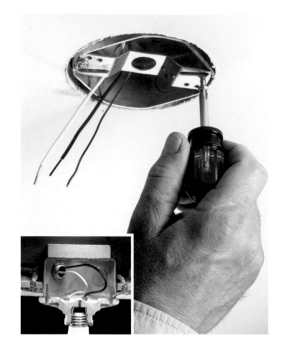

6 Now, take a look at the electrical box. Most fixtures installed in the last few decades are attached to a mounting strap, a strip of metal reaching from one side of the electrical box to another and attached with two screws. Older light fixtures were often mounted directly to the holes in the box (inset), a less safe installation that doesn't meet current electrical codes.

7 If the box doesn't have a mounting strap, attach one. One might be included with your new fixture; otherwise, you can buy one at any hardware store or home center.

8 You will probably find a bare copper wire in the box. Connect this wire to the screw near the center of the mounting strap. Wrap the wire clockwise around the screw and turn the screw until it is snug.

9 Set the new fixture on top of a ladder or have a helper support it. You'll find two short wires—called leads—coming from the fixture, one white and one black. If the ends of the leads are not already stripped, remove about ¾" of insulation from each wire end. Hold the white lead from the fixture next to the white wire from the ceiling. Push the ends into a wire connector, and twist the connector clockwise until it is snug.

10 Now connect the black wire to the black lead with a wire connector in the same way. Give both connections a gentle tug to make sure the connectors are tight.

11 Tuck the wire connections into the ceiling box on either side of the mounting strap. Hold the fixture over the electrical box so its two mounting holes line up with the holes on the mounting strap. Secure the light to the ceiling box by driving the fixture's mounting screws through the holes in the fixture base and into the strap. These screws are typically quite long, so an electric screwdriver is helpful.

SAFETY TIP

When picking a new ceiling fixture, select one with a bulb wattage rating appropriate to the bulb size you'll be using. For example, if you're installing a fixture that uses two bulbs, and you want to use 100-watt bulbs for maximum light, your fixture must be rated for 200 watts or more. A 120-watt fixture, on the other hand, can accept two 60-watt bulbs.

12 With the fixture secured to the box, you can install the lightbulbs and shades. Each fixture is a little different; follow the manufacturer's instructions. Once the bulbs are in, restore power to the fixture and test it.

20

Replace a Hanging Light Fixture

Replacing an old chandelier is a quick and easy way to make a big change to a room's character, not to mention the quality of its light.

CHANDELIERS AND OTHER HANGING FIXTURES EXIST IN A HUGE VARIETY OF STYLES, so chances are good that you might acquire a house with a chandelier you find less than attractive. Of course, you might also have a chandelier stop working for some reason. Either way, they're easy enough to replace.

A properly installed chandelier has more bracing behind it than a standard ceiling fixture, so don't try to replace a simple ceiling globe with a 50-pound chandelier. You'll likely find a broken chandelier on your dining room table if you do.

CHANDELIERS 101

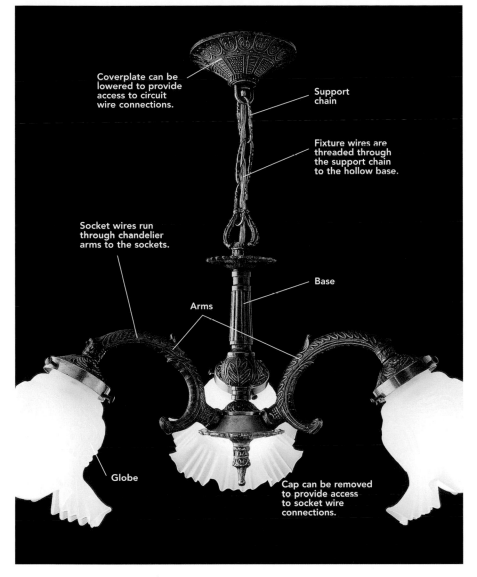

Coverplate can be lowered to provide access to circuit wire connections.

Support chain

Fixture wires are threaded through the support chain to the hollow base.

Socket wires run through chandelier arms to the sockets.

Base

Arms

Globe

Cap can be removed to provide access to socket wire connections.

Chandeliers can be a maze of wires, but fortunately, to install one, you only need to deal with the two fixture wires that snake up the chain.

HERE'S HOW

Heavy chandeliers and ceiling fans are suspended from electrical boxes that are secured between ceiling joists with heavy-duty braces.

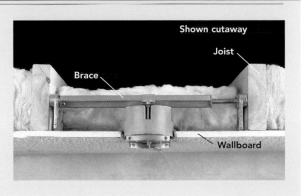

Shown cutaway

Joist

Brace

Wallboard

Combination tool

Screwdriver

Voltage sensor

Replacement chandelier

SKILLS YOU'LL NEED

• Making wire connections (page 12)

Note: This job is easier with two people.

DIFFICULTY LEVEL

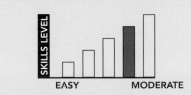

SKILLS LEVEL

EASY   MODERATE

Allow about 2 hours for this project.

HOW TO INSTALL A NEW CHANDELIER

Chandeliers are heavy, as you will learn very quickly when you're removing or installing one. It's better to rig up some means of temporary support for the fixture than to rely on a helper to hold it or—worse still—try to hold it yourself (you will need both hands to make the connections). One solution is to position a tall stepladder directly below the work area so you can rest the fixture on the top platform. And just in case the fixture falls, remove all the bulbs and globes before you do any of the work.

Retainer nut with integral chain loop

1 Remove the old light fixture. To gain access to the wiring connections, unfasten the retainer nut that secures the coverplate for the electrical box. On some chandeliers (such as the one above), the ring that holds the support chain for the chandelier is integral to the retainer nut, so unfastening it will mean the fixture is being supported only by the electrical wires.

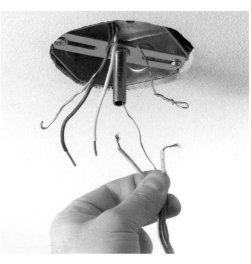

2 Turn off the power to the old fixture at the main service panel. Use a voltage sensor to verify that the circuit is dead. With the light switch turned on, insert the sensor's probe into the electrical box within ½" of the wires inside. If the sensor beeps or lights up, then the circuit is live and you've shut off the wrong circuit. Shut off additional circuits until the probe confirms that you've shut off the correct one.

3 Remove the wire connectors from all the wires in the box and separate the wires. If the support chain is still attached, unscrew the mounting nut from the end of the threaded nipple inside the box. Disconnect the bare copper wire from the screw near the center of the mounting strap. Pull the old wires down through the threaded nipple.

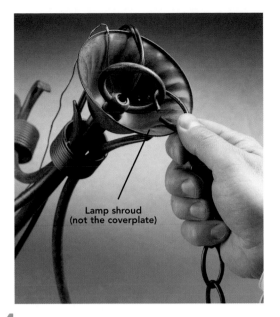

Lamp shroud
(not the coverplate)

4 Adjust the length of the support chain on the new chandelier (if necessary) so it will hang at the desired height when mounted. This is normally done by disconnecting the chain from the support ring on the fixture, removing the required number of links and then reattaching the chain.

5 There will be two insulated wires and a bare copper ground woven in with the chain on your new fixture. There should be 6" to 12" of extra wire at the top of the chain. If the ends of these wires aren't stripped, use your combination tool to strip away ¾" of insulation.

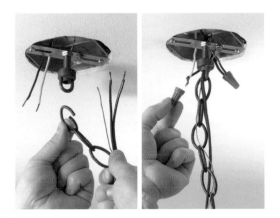

6 Hang the new fixture from the threaded nipple (unless the chain support nut is integral to the coverplate retainer, as in step 1). You may need to screw the threaded nipple farther into the mounting plate so it does not extend past the coverplate. Or, you may need to replace the mounting strap and nipple with correctly sized hardware (usually provided with the new fixture). Make the wire connections, including attaching the bare copper wire to the grounding screw on the mounting strap.

7 Carefully tuck the wires into the electrical box and then tighten the retainer for the coverplate so it is snug against the ceiling. Restore power and test the fixture.

21

Installing Track Lights

If you currently have a ceiling-mounted light fixture that is not meeting your lighting needs, it's simple to replace it with a track-lighting fixture. With track lighting you can easily change the type and number of lights, their position on the track, and the direction they aim. These fixtures come in many different styles, including short three-foot track systems with just one or two lights up to 12-foot systems with five or more lights.

TRACK LIGHTING OFFERS A BEAUTIFUL AND FUNCTIONAL WAY TO INCREASE THE AMOUNT OF LIGHT in a room or simply to update its look. A variety of fixture and lamp options lets you control the shape, color, and intensity of the light. Installing track lighting in place of an existing ceiling-mounted light fixture involves basic wiring and hand-tool skills, but the connections are even easier to make than with traditional light fixtures. Once installed, the system is very easy to upgrade or expand in the future.

TRACK LIGHTING 101

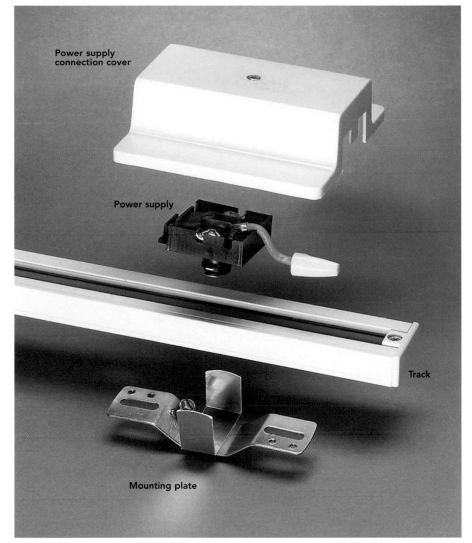

Power supply
connection cover

Power supply

Track

Mounting plate

Track systems include a lot of components, but fortunately you can buy all-inclusive starter kits containing everything you need for a basic installation, as well as a foundation for later upgrades if you wish.

TERMS YOU NEED TO KNOW

POWER SUPPLY—This little piece of hardware varies in appearance from kit to kit, but in all cases, it feeds power from the household wiring to the electrified pathways inside the track (and this powers the lights).

TOOLS & SUPPLIES YOU'LL NEED

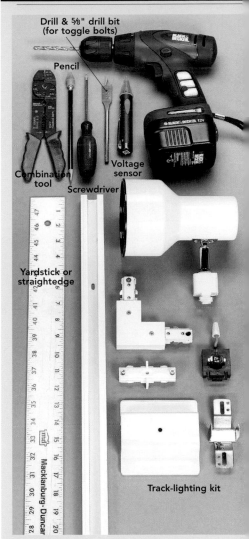

Drill & ⅝" drill bit
(for toggle bolts)

Pencil

Combination tool

Screwdriver

Voltage sensor

Yardstick or straightedge

Track-lighting kit

SKILLS YOU'LL NEED

- Turning off power (page 10)
- Testing for power (page 11)
- Making wire connections (page 12)
- Light carpentry skills

DIFFICULTY LEVEL

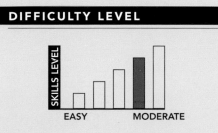

SKILLS LEVEL

EASY   MODERATE

This project will take about half a day.

1 Locate the breaker for the light circuit you're working on and switch that breaker into the OFF position. If you have an older electrical service panel, you may have glass fuses instead of breakers. If so, pull the fuse for that circuit. Close the cover of the breaker or fuse cabinet.

2 Remove the globe and the lightbulbs from the fixture. Detach the old light from the ceiling electrical box. Most fixtures use two long screws to secure the fixture base to the electrical box in the ceiling. Hold the fixture with one hand while you use a screwdriver to remove the two screws. Gently pull the light straight down, exposing the wiring.

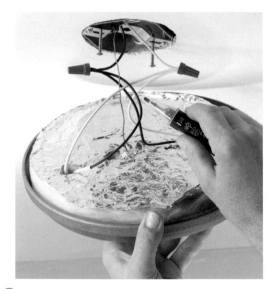

3 Use a voltage sensor to verify that the circuit is dead. Insert the sensor's probe into the electrical box within ½" of the black wires inside. If the sensor beeps or lights up, then the circuit is still live, and you'll need to trip the correct breaker to disconnect power to the fixture. If the sensor does not beep or light up, the circuit is dead and you can proceed safely.

4 Remove the fixture by disconnecting the wires. Use your hands to unscrew the wire connectors by turning them counterclockwise. After removing the wire connectors, pull the fixture completely away from the box (you can recycle it or save it). If you need to stop working and restore the power, first separate the wires coming from the ceiling box and cap them each with a wire connector.

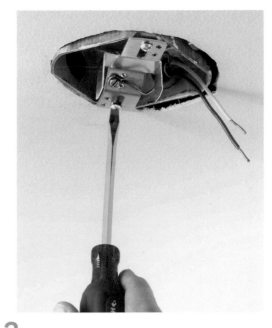

1 Turn off power (step 1, opposite page). Thread the three wires from the power supply hardware through the hole in the center of the mounting plate. Connect the power supply wires using wire connectors (the kit will come with them). The green wire on the power supply is connected to the bare copper wire coming out of the electrical box. Connect the white and black wires from the power supply to the white wire and black wires coming from the electrical box in the same way.

2 Carefully tuck the wires back up into the ceiling box and attach the mounting plate using the screws provided with the kit. The power supply can simply hang by its wires for the time being.

WHAT IF...?

What if the track is too long? Most types of track can be cut to length easily with a hacksaw. Use a saw fitted with a sharp blade and make a straight cut.

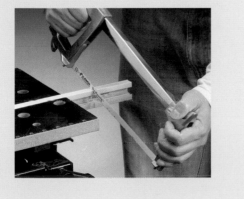

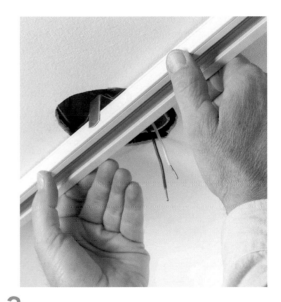

3 Draw a reference line on the ceiling to mark the track's path from the mounting plate to the end of the track. If possible, position the track directly underneath a ceiling joist so you can screw it to the joists. Otherwise, you will need to use toggle bolts to hold the tracks in the ceiling. Snap the track temporarily onto the mounting plate so it follows the reference line.

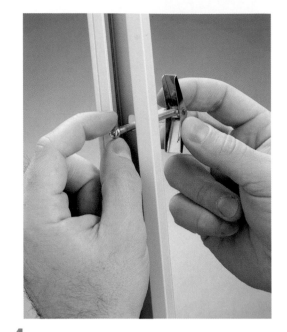

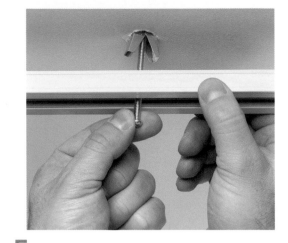

4 Mark the screw hole locations on the ceiling by making a dot through each hole in the track. After you mark the screw locations, remove the track and drill holes in the ceiling for the mounting screws. Begin by threading the bolts onto the track. First, unscrew the toggle bolt from the spring-loaded wings. Insert the toggle bolts through the holes in the track. Hold the wing on the ceiling-side of the track, then screw the bolt back into the toggle wings with two or three turns of the bolt.

5 Drill holes slightly larger then the thickness of the closed toggle wings. Pinch the wings of one toggle together and push it into the hole in the ceiling. The wings will snap open once they enter the cavity and hold the bolt in place. Push the other toggle bolts into their holes in the same way. Once all the bolts for a track section are in their holes, fit the track end to the mounting plate, and then tighten all the toggle bolts. Tighten the two screws on the mounting plate.

HERE'S HOW

Here's how to add another section of track. You can link sections of track together with connectors (your kit may include some or you can buy them separately, along with additional track sections). Connector pieces will also allow you to make 90-degree turns or T's on your track path. The connectors snap into the end of the track and are secured with screws.

6 Now you can connect the power supply to the track. Insert the power supply into the track and twist the connector until it snaps securely into place (connector installation may vary by manufacturer). The connector is made so that it cannot be snapped in the wrong way, so you'll know when it's in correctly. Attach the white and black wires to the screw terminals on the power supply.

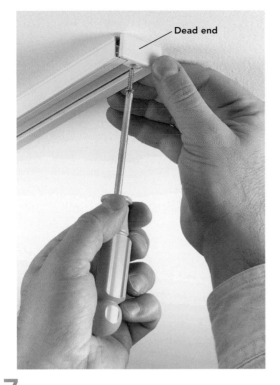

Dead end

7 Most kits will require you to cap the open ends of track dead ends. Snap them onto the ends of track pieces and secure them with screws.

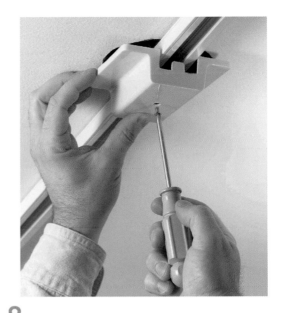

8 Now you can fit the decorative cover over the mounting plate. It may snap in place or be secured with screws. This will cover up the mounting plate completely.

9 You can begin inserting the light heads into the track at this point. These should simply twist-lock into place. Turn on power and test the light head.

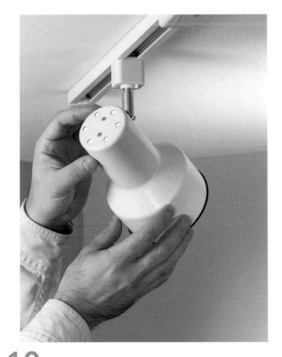

10 If the light works, locate a position you like and push down the locking tab on the side of the fixture to secure the light in this location. Install appropriate bulbs in the light sockets, according to the manufacturer's instructions. Install the remaining heads.

Installing a
Motion-sensing Floodlight

22

An exterior floodlight with a motion sensor is an effective security measure.
Make sure you keep the motion sensor adjusted so it doesn't give false alarms.

MOST HOUSES AND GARAGES HAVE FLOODLIGHTS ON THEIR EXTERIORS. You can easily upgrade these fixtures so that they provide additional security by replacing them with motion-sensing floodlights. Motion-sensing floods can be set up to detect motion in a specific area—like a walkway or driveway—and then cast light into that area. And there are few things intruders like less than the spotlight. These lights typically have timers that allow you to control how long the light stays on and photosensors that prevent the light from coming on during the day.

FLOODLIGHTS 101

Eye

B

A

C

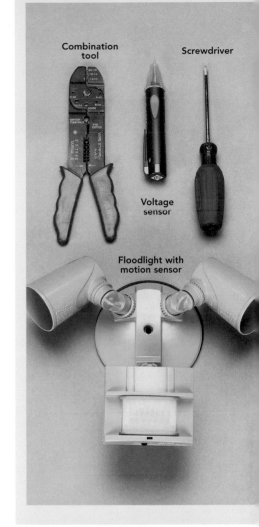

Combination tool

Screwdriver

Voltage sensor

Floodlight with motion sensor

A motion-sensing light fixture provides inexpensive and effective protection against intruders. It has an infrared eye that triggers the light fixture when a moving object crosses its path. Choose a light fixture with: a photo cell (A) to prevent the light from turning on in daylight; an adjustable timer (B) to control how long the light stays on; and range control (C) to adjust the reach of the motion-sensor eye.

SKILLS YOU'LL NEED

- Turning off the power (page 10)
- Testing for power (page 11)
- Making wire connections (page 12)

HERE'S HOW

Here's how to make sure no one accidentally turns off your security lights—or any other light you don't want turned off. Switch locks are inexpensive plastic covers that lock a switch in the ON or OFF position. You can find them at any hardware store or home center.

DIFFICULTY LEVEL

EASY

MODERATE

This project will take about 1 hour.

1 Turn off power to the old fixture. To remove it, unscrew the mounting screws on the part of the fixture attached to the wall. There will probably be four of them. Carefully pull the fixture away from the wall, exposing the wires. Don't touch the wires yet.

2 Before you touch any wires, use a voltage sensor to verify that the circuit is dead. With the light switch turned ON, insert the sensor's probe into the electrical box and hold the probe within ½" of the wires inside to confirm that there is no voltage flow. Disconnect the wire connectors and remove the old fixture.

3 Examine the ends of the three wires coming from the box (one white, one black, and one bare copper). They should be clean and free of corrosion. If the ends are in poor condition, clip them off and then strip ¾" of wire insulation with a combination tool.

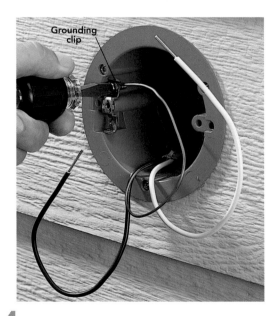

Grounding clip

4 If the electrical box is nonmetallic and does not have a metal grounding clip, install a grounding clip or replace the box with one that does have a clip and make sure the ground wire is attached to it securely. Some light fixtures have a grounding terminal on the base. If yours has one, attach the grounding wire from the house directly to the terminal.

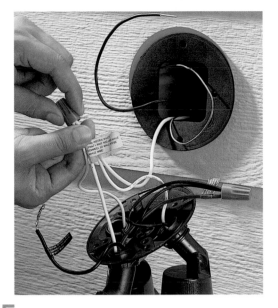

5 Now you can attach the new fixture. Begin by sliding a rubber or foam gasket (usually provided with the fixture) over the wires and onto the flange of the electrical box. Set the new fixture on top of a ladder or have a helper hold it while you make the wiring connections. There may be as many as three white wires coming from the fixture. Join all white wires, including the feed wire from the house, using a wire connector.

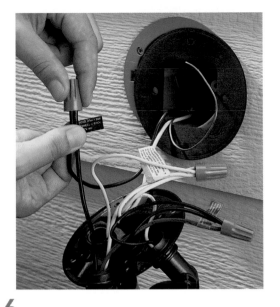

6 Next, join the black wire from the box and the single black wire from the fixture with a wire connector. You may see a couple of black wires and a red wire already joined on the fixture. You can ignore these in your installation.

7 Neatly tuck all the wires into the box so they are behind the gasket. Align the holes in the gasket with the holes in the box, and then position the fixture over the gasket so its mounting holes are also aligned with the gasket. Press the fixture against the gasket and drive the four mounting screws into the box. Install floodlight bulbs (exterior rated) and restore power.

8 Test the fixture. You will still be able to turn it on and off with the light switch inside. Flip the switch to ON and pass your hand in front of the motion sensor. The light should come on. Adjust the motion sensor to cover the traffic areas and pivot the light head to illuminate the intended area.

23

Repairing Fluorescent Light Fixtures

Troubleshooting a fluorescent light that's flickering or won't work is a process of testing and checking that begins with inspecting the fluorescent tubes to make sure they're making good contact with the fixture sockets and are in good condition.

FLUORESCENT FIXTURES ARE GREAT LIGHTING CHOICES because they save energy and offer many different quality-of-light options, from the hue and color of the light to its brightness. And fluorescent lamps have a much longer life than regular incandescent lamps. But as fluorescent fixtures age, small parts begin to fail. Replacing the tubes is easy, and replacing the ballast (a transformer-type part that distributes power to the sockets) is only slightly more difficult. But if the fixture is old it may make more sense to replace the entire fixture with a newer (and probably quieter) model.

FLUORESCENT LIGHTS 101

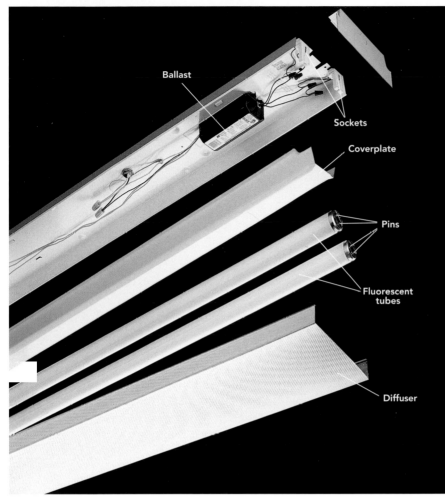

Ballast

Sockets

Coverplate

Pins

Fluorescent tubes

Diffuser

Fluorescent fixtures come in lots of different lengths, from 6 inches to 6 feet. They all work basically the same. The fixture consists of a diffuser and a coverplate and housing that contain a ballast that connects to the sockets that hold the tubes.

BUYER'S TIP

Here's how to buy a fluorescent tube: You'll need three pieces of information: the length of the tube, the end type, and the wattage. There are a couple different styles of pin configuration for the ends of tubes. The two-pin style shown here is most common, but there are others. If yours looks different, take it with you to the hardware store to find an exact match. The wattage of the fluorescent tube will be printed somewhere along its length. Buy a new tube with the same watt rating. For best value, buy fluorescent tubes in multiple tube packs, as you would with other types of lightbulbs.

TOOLS & SUPPLIES YOU'LL NEED

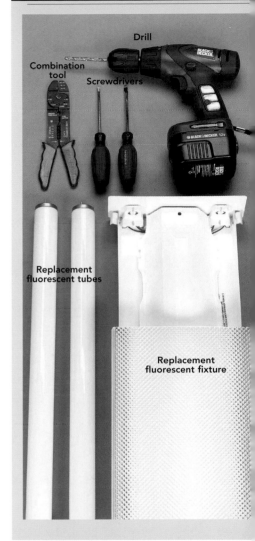

Drill

Combination tool

Screwdrivers

Replacement fluorescent tubes

Replacement fluorescent fixture

SKILLS YOU'LL NEED

- Turning off power (page 10)
- Testing for power (page 11)
- Making wire connections (page 12)

Note: This may be easier with two people.

DIFFICULTY LEVEL

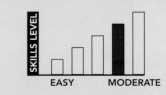

SKILLS LEVEL

EASY   MODERATE

Allow about 2 hours for this project.

HOW TO REPLACE A FLUORESCENT TUBE

1 If your fluorescent light is flickering or not working, check the tubes first. Start by removing the plastic diffuser that covers the light so you can access the florescent tubes. The diffuser normally snaps into place. Squeeze it slightly at its sides to remove it.

2 Twist the tubes to confirm that they are seated correctly in the sockets. If they are securely in the sockets but the light won't light, remove the tubes by rotating them a quarter turn in each direction and pulling down.

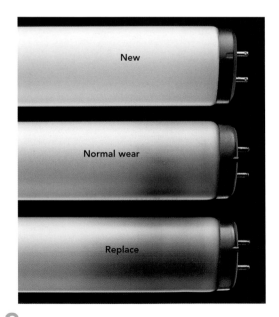

New

Normal wear

Replace

3 Take a look at the ends of the bulb. A little light gray coloring at the ends of a used fluorescent bulb is normal. But if one or more of the tube ends is blackened, the tube should be replaced.

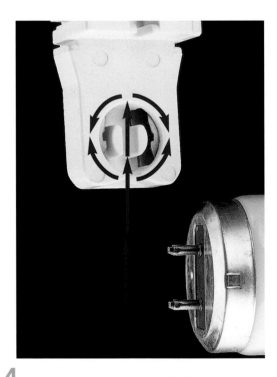

4 Purchase a replacement tube (see page 121) and install the new tubes by holding the tube so the pins are vertical. Slide the pins into the grooves in the sockets and push up. Then, turn the tube a quarter turn in each direction. Replace the diffuser and test the fixture.

HOW TO REPLACE A BALLAST

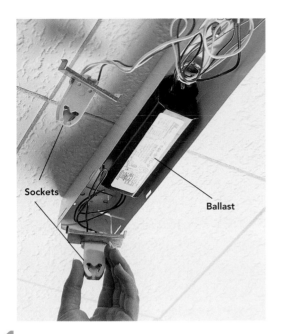

Sockets

Ballast

1 Turn off the power at the main service panel, then remove the diffuser, fluorescent tube, and coverplate. Test for power. Remove the sockets from the fixture housing by sliding them out, or by removing the mounting screws and lifting the sockets out.

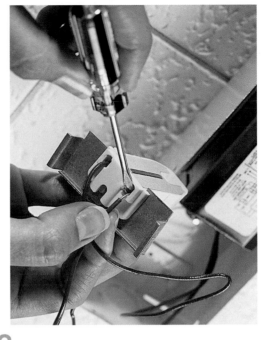

2 Disconnect the wires that lead from the ballast to the sockets by pushing a small screwdriver into the release openings (as seen above) or loosening the screw terminals. On some socket styles you'll need to cut the wires to within 2" of the socket to remove the ballast.

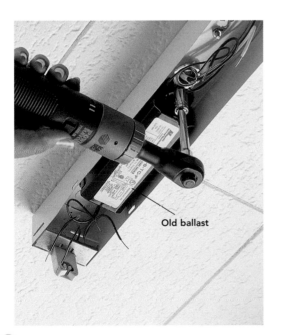

Old ballast

3 Remove the old ballast, using a ratchet wrench or screwdriver. Make sure to support the ballast so it does not fall (a little duct tape will do the job).

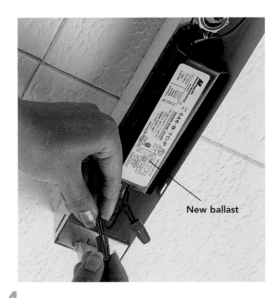

New ballast

4 Install a new ballast that has the same ratings as the old ballast. Attach the ballast wires to the socket wires and reinstall the coverplate, fluorescent tube, and diffuser. Turn on power to the light fixture at the main service panel.

HOW TO REPLACE A FLUORESCENT FIXTURE

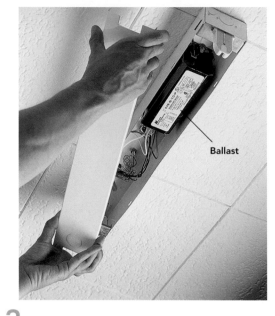

Ballast

1 If replacing the tube or ballast doesn't fix the problem, it's best to replace the whole light fixture. Start by removing the diffuser and the tubes. Then, turn off the power to the fixture at the service panel and test with a voltage tester.

2 Loosen the screws at each end of the metal coverplate on the fixture. If there are no screws, you may be able to remove the cover by pinching its ends and pulling down. Pull the coverplate free and set it aside.

BUYER'S TIP

How to buy a new fluorescent fixture: Look for a fixture of the same length and with the same number of tubes as the one you're replacing. You'll also want one rated for the same number of watts as your old one. The watt rating will be printed somewhere on the inside of the fixture.

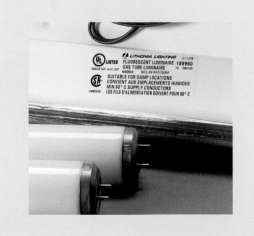

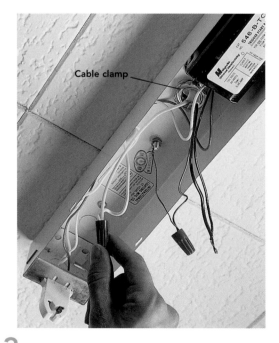

Cable clamp

3 Disconnect the fixture by unscrewing the wire connectors inside the fixture housing. Straighten out the three wires feeding into the fixture through the cable clamp and then unscrew the cable clamp.

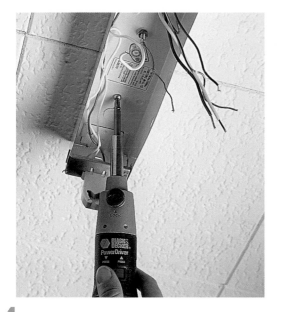

4 You can now completely remove the fixture by unscrewing the mounting screws. It's a good idea to have a helper support the fixture as you undo the screws. Move the fixture away from the ceiling, pulling the three wires through the hole.

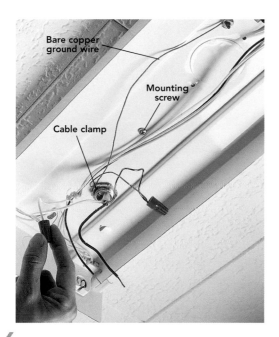

6 Attach the fixture to the ceiling with screws or toggle bolts driven up through mounting screw holes in the top of the fixture, and then tighten a retaining nut around the cable clamp. Make the wire connections (white to white, black to black, bare copper ground to grounding screw on fixture).

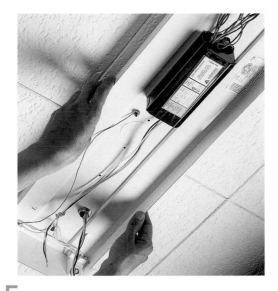

5 Remove the coverplate from the new fixture. On the bottom of the new fixture, you'll find several knockout holes. Remove a knockout that will fall under the electrical box in the ceiling when the fixture is installed (drive a screwdriver through the knockout to remove it). Attach a cable clamp in the knockout hole and feed the three wires from the ceiling box through the cable clamp as you raise the fixture up against the ceiling.

7 Reattach the coverplate on the new fixture, install the fluorescent tubes and snap in the diffuser. Restore power and test the fixture.

24

Fixing a Ceiling Fan

Even ceiling fans that are operated only occasionally are prone to failure or problems like excess wobble. Following the steps in this chapter will help you diagnose and solve common ceiling fan maladies.

CEILING FANS THAT WORK PROPERLY WILL SAVE MONEY on heating and cooling costs and add to the comfort of your home. But over time ceiling fans can fail to work, become noisy, the blades may wobble, or the pull-chain switch may become unreliable or just plain faulty. Before putting many hours of time and hard labor—not to mention the expense—into a new fan installation, diagnose the old fan to see if it can be easily repaired using these steps. Keep in mind that most consumer-level ceiling fans will never be completely silent when the fan is operating—moving air does make some noise, after all.

CEILING FANS 101

Mounting bracket

Canopy

Motor

Fan blades

Switch housing

Pull chain

Bottom cap

A ceiling fan is suspended from a sturdy mounting bracket and the connection is concealed by a decorative canopy.

FAN NOT WORKING? TRY THIS FIRST:

1 Make sure that the wall switch that controls the ceiling fan is in the ON position. Reach up to the fan and move the fan direction switch back and forth to confirm that it is fully engaged in one of the two positions (clockwise blade movement for summer, counterclockwise for winter). If the fan blades do not start rotating, even though the switch feels secure in one of the two positions, go to step 2.

2 Put your hand on the switch housing to feel for vibration. If a vibration or humming is present, the fan motor is malfunctioning and you should consider replacing the entire unit. No hum or vibration? Proceed to the further diagnostics beginning on page 128.

Fan direction switch

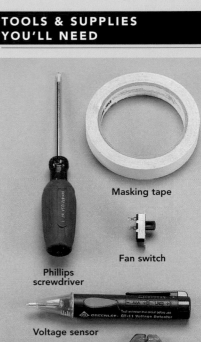

Masking tape

Fan switch

Phillips screwdriver

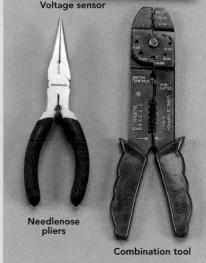

Voltage sensor

Needlenose pliers

Combination tool

SKILLS YOU'LL NEED

- Turning off power (page 10)
- Testing for power (page 11)
- Making wire connections (page 12)

DIFFICULTY LEVEL

SKILLS LEVEL

EASY   MODERATE

Allow 2 to 4 hours, and work with a helper.

HOW TO FIX A CEILING FAN

1 A leading cause of fan failure is loose wire connections. To inspect these connections, first shut off the power to the fan. Remove the fan blades to gain access, then remove the canopy that covers the ceiling box and fan mounting bracket. Most canopies are secured with screws on the outside shell. Have a helper hold the fan while you remove the screws so it won't fall.

2 Once the canopy is lowered, you'll see black, white, green, copper, and possibly blue wires. Hold a voltage sensor within ½" of these wires with the wall switch that controls the fan in the ON position. The black and blue wires should cause the sensor to beep if power is present.

HERE'S HOW

One common problem with older ceiling fans is that over time or due to incorrect initial installation, the blades begin to wobble as they spin. If you're within earshot, the vibration from wobbling is irritating, but it can also damage the fan and shorten its life. Wobbling has three main causes: (1) the fan blades may not be balanced properly, (2) the fan may not be tightly secured to the ceiling fan box, or (3) one or more of the fan blades may have become warped. Fixing any of these situations requires minimal effort and time.

1 Start by checking and tightening all hardware used to attach the blades to the mounting arms and the mounting arms to the motor. Hardware tends to loosen over time and this is frequently the cause of wobble.

2 If wobble persists, try switching around two of the blades. Often, this is all it takes to get the fan back into balance. If a blade is damaged or warped, try to locate a replacement blade.

3 If you still have wobble, turn the power off at the panel, remove the fan canopy, and inspect the mounting brace and the connection between the mounting pole and the fan motor. Tighten any loose connections and replace the canopy.

3 When you have confirmed that there is no power, check all the wire connections to make certain each is tight and making good contact. You may be able to see that a connection has come apart and needs to be remade. But even if you see one bad connection, check them all by gently tugging on the wire connectors. If the wires pull out of the wire connector or the connection feels loose, unscrew the wire connector from the wires.

4 Twist the wires back together the same way you found them, making sure the bare wires are making good contact with each other. Secure them with a new wire twist connector.

HERE'S HOW

Bad wiring connections often are caused by failed wire connectors. Inspect connections for signs of burning, corrosion, or rust. If the inside of any wire connector does not look clean and shiny, replace it with a new connector of the same size.

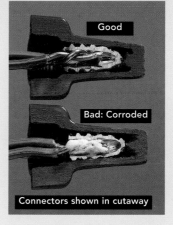

Good

Bad: Corroded

Connectors shown in cutaway

5 If everything works, reinstall the canopy by replacing the screws that were holding it in place. Reattach the fan blades and then restore power. If all connections are secure but the fan still doesn't work, try replacing the pull chain to resolve the problem (see next page).

HOW TO REPLACE A PULL-CHAIN SWITCH

1 Turn off the power at the main service panel. Use a screwdriver to remove the three to four screws that secure the bottom cap on the fan switch housing. Lower the cap to expose the wires that supply power to the pull-chain switch.

2 Test the wires by placing a voltage sensor within ½" of the wires. If the sensor beeps or lights up, then the circuit is still live, and is not safe to work. When the sensor does not beep or light up, the circuit is dead and may be worked upon.

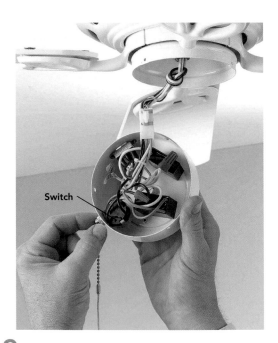

Switch

3 Locate the switch unit (the part that the pull chain used to be attached to if it broke off); it's probably made of plastic. You'll need to replace the whole switch. Fan switches are connected with from three to eight wires, depending on the number of speed settings.

4 Attach a small piece of tape to each wire that enters the switch and write an identifying number on the tape. Start at one side of the switch and label the wires in the order they're attached.

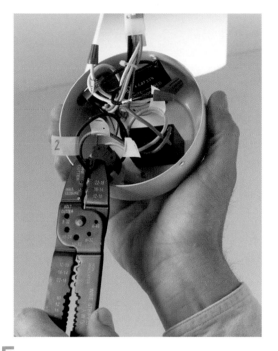

5 Disconnect the old switch wires, in most cases by cutting the wires off as close to the old switch as possible. Unscrew the retaining nut that secures the switch to the switch housing.

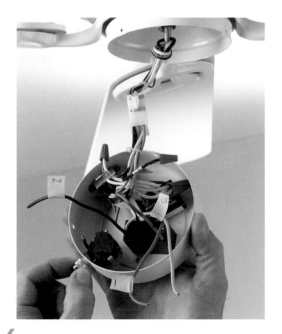

6 Remove the switch. There may be one or two screws that hold it in place or it may be secured to the outside of the fan with a small, knurled nut, which you can loosen with needlenose pliers. Purchase an identical new switch.

BUYER'S TIP

Here's how to buy a new switch. Bring the old switch to the hardware store or home center, and find an identical new switch—one with the same number and color of wires. It should also attach to the fan motor wires in the same way (slots or screw terminals or with integral wires and wire connectors) and that attaches to the fan in the same way. If you are unable to locate an identical switch, find the owners manual for your ceiling fan and contact the manufacturer. Or, find the brand and model number of the fan and order a switch from a ceiling fan dealer or electronics supply store.

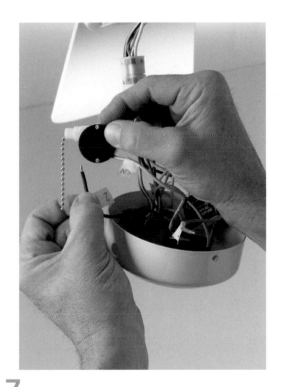

7 Connect the new switch using the same wiring configuration as on the old model. To make connections, first use a wire stripper to strip ¾" of insulation from the ends of each of the wires coming from the fan motor (the ones you cut in step 5). Attach the wires to the new switch in the same order and configuraion as they were attached to the old switch. Secure the new switch in the housing and make sure all wires are tucked neatly inside. Reattach the bottom cap. Test all the fan's speeds to make sure all the connections are good.

Extra Credit:
Installing Raceway Wiring

25

Raceway wiring systems are surface-mounted networks of electrical boxes and hollow metal tracks that allow you to expand an existing wiring circuit without cutting into your walls.

SURFACE WIRING CAN BE USED TO EXTEND POWER FROM ANY EXISTING RECEPTACLE to another location without cutting into walls, floors, or ceilings. If you're relying on an ugly (not to mention dangerous) tangle of extension cords to compensate for a shortage of proper receptacles, a raceway system of surface wiring may be your solution. Surface wiring uses inconspicuous metal channels that are mounted to the walls. The channels are easily removed and can be extended again or rerouted as your needs change.

RACEWAYS 101

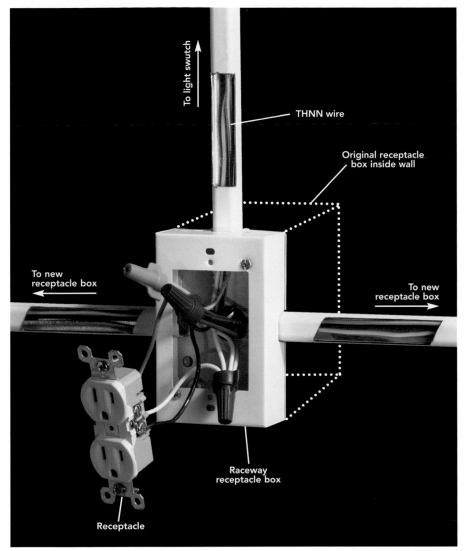

To light switch

THNN wire

Original receptacle
box inside wall

To new
receptacle box

To new
receptacle box

Receptacle
box

Raceway
receptacle box

Receptacle

The raceway receptacle box is mounted directly to the original electrical box (usually for a receptacle) and raceway tracks are attached to it. The tracks house THNN wires that run from the raceway box to new receptacles and light switches.

HERE'S HOW

Here's how to determine if an electrical circuit has enough capacity for you to add a new receptacle or light. Count the number of receptacles and lights that are already part of the circuit. Multiply this number by 1.5 amps. The result should not exceed the amperage of the circuit (usually 15 or 20 amps). The 1.5 amps estimate is for everyday small appliances, lamps, and lighting. Do not add onto a circuit if it supplies or is intended to supply power to high-draw appliances such as a refrigerator, microwave oven, or electric heater. Overloading a circuit is unsafe and will cause the circuit breaker to trip. It's always a good idea to consult your local electrical inspector before you start.

TOOLS & SUPPLIES YOU'LL NEED

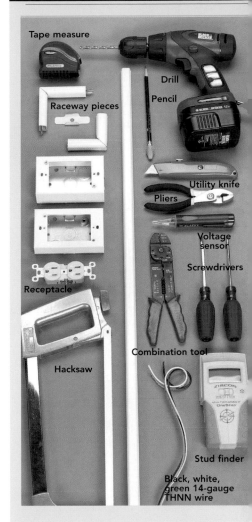

Tape measure

Raceway pieces

Drill

Pencil

Utility knife

Pliers

Voltage sensor

Screwdrivers

Receptacle

Combination tool

Hacksaw

Stud finder

Black, white, green 14-gauge THNN wire

SKILLS YOU'LL NEED

- Turning off power (page 10)
- Testing for power (page 11)
- Making wire connections (page 12)
- Light carpentry skills

DIFFICULTY LEVEL

SKILLS LEVEL

EASY   MODERATE

Allow half a day for this project.

1 Confirm that the circuit you want to expand will support a new receptacle or light (see page 133). Mark the planned location of the new receptacle or switch on the wall and mea-sure to the nearest existing receptacle. Purchase enough raceway to cover this distance plus about 10 percent extra. Buy a surface-mounted starter box, new receptacle box, and fittings for your project (the raceway product packaging usually provides guidance for shopping).

2 First shut off the power to the switch. Remove the coverplate from the receptacle by unscrewing the screw that holds the plate to the electrical box. Set the screws and the plate aside. With the coverplate off, you will be able to see the receptacle and the electrical box it is attached to.

3 Before you remove the old receptacle, use a voltage sensor to double-check that the circuit is dead. Hold your voltage sensor's probe within ½" of the wires on each side of the receptacle. If the sensor beeps or lights up, then the receptacle is still live, and you'll need to trip the correct breaker to disconnect power to the receptacle. If the sensor does not beep or light up, the receptacle is dead and you can proceed safely.

4 Remove the receptacle from the box by unscrewing the two long screws that hold the switch to the box. Once the screws are out, gently pull the receptacle away from the box. It won't pull away easily, since the wires are still attached, so pull firmly. Depending on how your receptacle has been wired, you may find two insulated wires and a bare copper wire or four insulated wires and a bare wire. Detach these wires and set the receptacle aside.

5 Your starter box includes a box and a mounting plate with a hole in its center. Pull all the wires you just disconnected through the hole, taking care not to scrape them on the edges of the hole. Screw the mounting plate to the existing receptacle box with the included mounting screws.

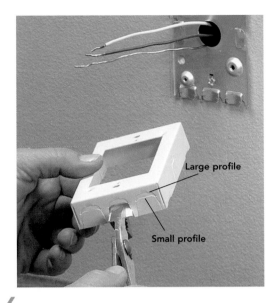

Large profile

Small profile

6 Remove a knockout from the starter box to create an opening for the raceway track, using pliers. Often, the prepunched knockouts have two profile options—make sure the knockout you remove matches the profile of your track.

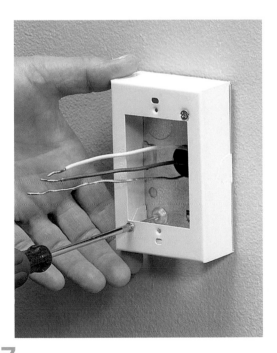

7 Hold the box portion of the starter box over the mounting plate on the existing receptacle. Drive the mounting screws through the holes in the box and into the threaded openings in the mounting plate.

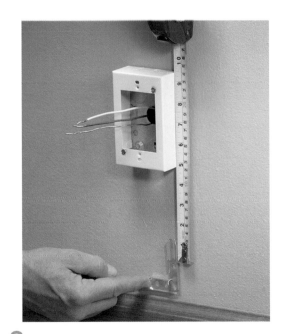

8 Set the mounting bracket for an elbow connector ¼" above the baseboard (having the track run along the baseboard edge looks better than running it in a straight line out of the starter box). Measure from the knockout in the starter box to the top of the bracket and cut a piece of raceway ½" longer than this measurement.

Here's how to cut metal raceway. Secure the track in a vise or clamping work support and cut with a hacksaw. Make sure the mounting bracket and the track cover are aligned at the end and cut through both at the same time. For best results, use long, slow strokes and don't bear down too hard on the saw.

Here's how to install wall anchors. Mark screw locations on the wall, then drill ¼" holes through the wall at the marks. Tap a plastic wall anchor into the hole with a hammer so the underside of the top flange is flush against the surface of the wall. When a screw is driven into the wall anchor sleeve, the sleeve will expand in the hole and hold the screw securely.

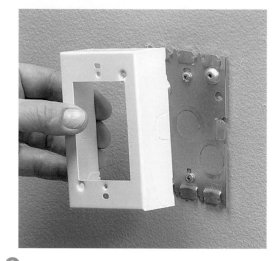

9 At the new receptacle location, use a laser level to transfer the height of the top of the starter box and mark a reference line. If possible, locate the box so at least one screw hole in the mounting plate falls over a wall stud. Position the mounting plate for the receptacle box up against the laser line and secure it with screws driven through the mounting plate holes. If the plate is not located over a wall stud, use wall anchors (see below left).

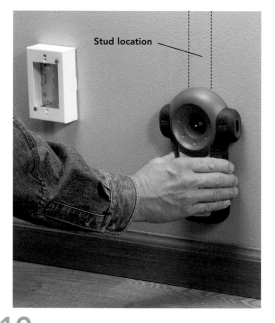

Stud location

10 Use a stud finder to locate and mark all of the wall framing members between the old receptacle and the new one. There should be a stud every 16" along the wall, and the studs should be about 1½" wide.

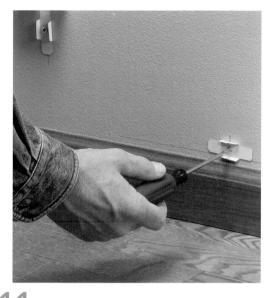

11 At stud locations, use a laser level as a reference for marking a line ¼" above the top of the baseboard. Attach mounting clips for the raceway track at these marks.

12 Install mounting clips ½" or so below the knockouts on both the starter box and the new receptacle box. The clips should line up with the knockouts.

13 At the starter box slide one end of the short piece of raceway into the knockout so that about ⅛" extends into the box. Snap the raceway into the clip below the knockout. Repeat this same procedure at the new receptacle box. Slip a bushing (included with installation kit) over the ends of the tracks where they enter the box.

14 The elbow piece will have two parts, a mounting plate and a cap. Install the mounting plates directly below the pieces of track entering the receptacle boxes.

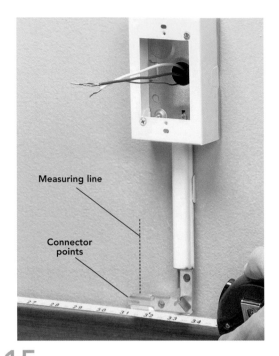

Measuring line

Connector points

15 Now you can measure and cut the long piece of raceway that fits between the two receptacles. Measure the distance between the ends of the horizontal parts of the elbows, and cut a length of raceway to that length. Be sure to measure all the way to the base of the clip, not just to the tips of the connector points.

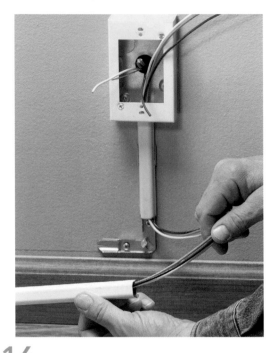

16 Cut black, white, and green THNN wire about 2-ft. longer than the length of each wiring run. Snake the end of each wire into the starter box, through the knockout, and into the vertical raceway. Then snake the wire all the way through the long piece of raceway so about 12" to 16" come out on each side.

WHAT IF...?

What if I need to go around a corner? Use corner pieces to guide raceway around corners. Corners are available for inside or outside corners and consist of a mounting plate and a cap piece. Inside corners may be used at wall/ceiling junctures.

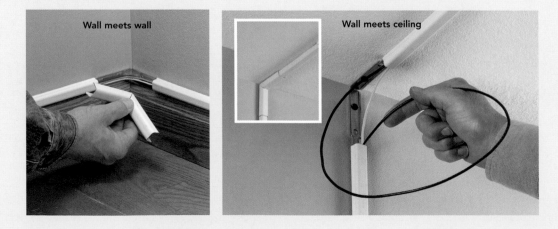

Wall meets wall

Wall meets ceiling

WHAT IF...?

What if I need a piece of raceway track that's longer than the longest piece available at the hardware store (usually 5 ft.)?

You can use straight connector pieces to join two lengths of raceway. Much like an elbow piece, they have a mounting plate and a cover that snaps over the wiring.

17 Now you can snap the long piece of raceway into the mounting clips. Line one end of the raceway up with the end of an elbow and begin pressing the raceway into the clips until it is snapped into all of the clips. At the new receptacle location, snake the ends of the wires up through the vertical piece of raceway and into the new receptacle box. There should be about 6" of wire coming out at each box.

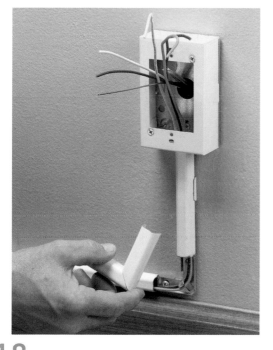

18 Finish the raceway by snapping the elbow cover pieces into place over the mounting plates, one at the starter box and another at the new receptacle location. You may need to rap the plate with a rubber mallet to get enough force to snap it on. Make sure all of the wire fits completely within the cover pieces.

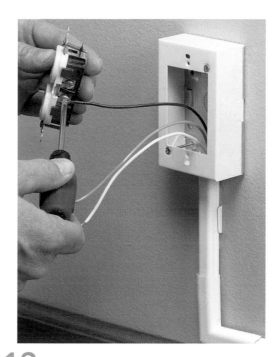

19 Now you can wire the receptacles. Begin at the new receptacle location. Take the black wire and wrap the end of the wire around the bottom gold screw on the side of the receptacle. Tighten the screw so it's snug.

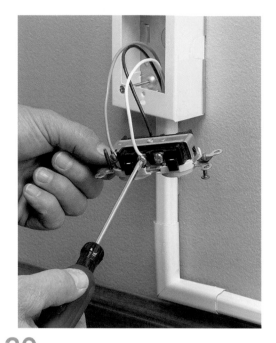

20 Now take the white wire and wrap the end of the wire around the silver screw opposite the copper one you just used. Tighten the screw so it's snug. Connect the green wire to the green-colored screw on the bottom of the receptacle.

21 Once the connections are made, gently tuck the wires and the receptacle into the box so the holes in the top and bottom of the receptacle align with the holes in the box. Use a screwdriver to drive the two long mounting screws that hold the receptacle to the box. Attach the cover plate.

22 Now you can reinstall the old receptacle (or a replacement) at the starter box. First, make sure the power is still off with your voltage tester. Take the old black wire and wrap the end of the wire around the top gold screw on the side of the receptacle. Tighten the screw so it's snug.

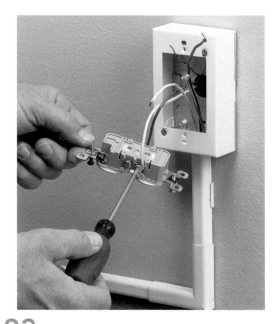

23 Take the old white wire and wrap the end of the wire around the silver screw opposite the copper one you just used. Tighten the screw so it's snug.

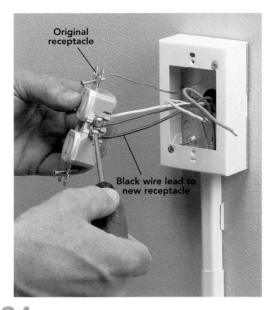

Original receptacle

Black wire lead to new receptacle

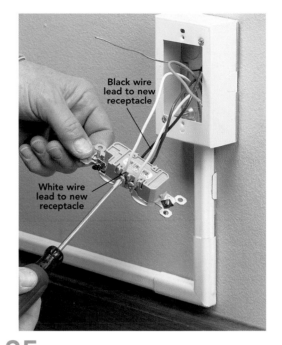

Black wire lead to new receptacle

White wire lead to new receptacle

24 The next step connects the old receptacle to the new one. Take the black wire that goes into the raceway and wrap the end of the wire around the bottom gold screw on the side of the receptacle. Tighten the screw so it's snug.

25 Take the old white wire and wrap the end of the wire around the silver screw opposite the copper one you just used. Tighten the screw so it's snug.

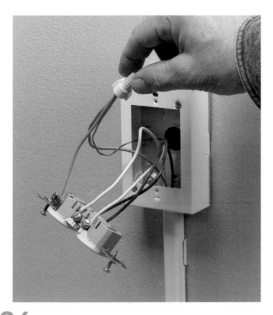

26 Finally, cut a piece of green wire about 6" long and strip ¾" from both ends (this is called a pigtail wire). Join one end of the pigtail with the ends of the bare and green wires in the box, using a wire connector. Wrap the other end of the pigtail around the green screw on the receptacle. Tighten the screw until it's snug.

27 Once the connections are made, gently tuck the wires and the receptacle into the box so the holes in the top and bottom of the receptacle align with the holes in the box. Use a screwdriver to drive the two long mounting screws that hold the receptacle to the box. Install the coverplate. You can now restore the power and test your new receptacle.

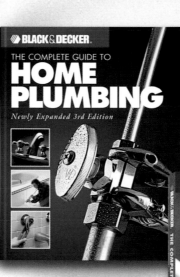
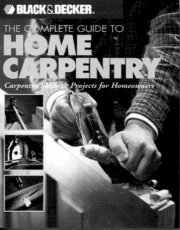
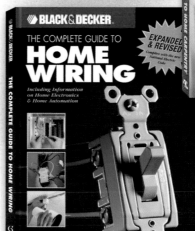

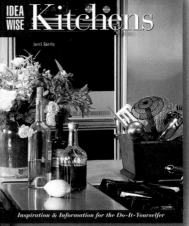